1st EDITION

Perspectives on Modern World History

The Crisis in Darfur

1st EDITION

Perspectives on Modern World History

The Crisis in Darfur

Jeff Hay

Book Editor

GREENHAVEN PRESS
A part of Gale, Cengage Learning

GALE
CENGAGE Learning

Detroit • New York • San Francisco • New Haven, Conn • Waterville, Maine • London

Christine Nasso, *Publisher*
Elizabeth Des Chenes, *Managing Editor*

© 2011 Greenhaven Press, a part of Gale, Cengage Learning.

Gale and Greenhaven Press are registered trademarks used herein under license.

For more information, contact:
Greenhaven Press
27500 Drake Rd.
Farmington Hills, MI 48331-3535
Or you can visit our Internet site at gale.cengage.com.

For product information and technology assistance, contact us at
Gale Customer Support, 1-800-877-4253.

For permission to use material from this text or product, submit all requests online at
www.cengage.com/permissions.

Further permissions questions can be e-mailed to permissionrequest@cengage.com.

Articles in Greenhaven Press anthologies are often edited for length to meet page requirements. In addition, original titles of these works are changed to clearly present the main thesis and to explicitly indicate the author's opinion. Every effort is made to ensure that Greenhaven Press accurately reflects the original intent of the authors. Every effort has been made to trace the owners of copyrighted material.

Cover image Custom Medical Stock Photo, Inc. Reproduced by permission.

LIBRARY OF CONGRESS CATALOGING-IN-PUBLICATION DATA

The crisis in Darfur / Jeff Hay, book editor.
    p. cm. -- (Perspectives on modern world history)
    Includes bibliographical references and index.
    ISBN 978-0-7377-5257-1 (hardcover)
    1. Sudan--History--Darfur Conflict, 2003---Juvenile literature. I. Hay, Jeff.
    DT159.6.D27.C76 2011
    962.404'3--dc22
                                        2010033168

Printed in the United States of America
1 2 3 4 5 6 7 14 13 12 11 10

CONTENTS

A scholar of Africa suggests that arguments over whether the chaos in Darfur can be termed a genocide may be important for institutions and academics but are largely distractions, making it easier to ignore the experiences of the hundreds of thousands of victims.

China's interest in Sudanese oil and other resources has helped spur an economic boom in parts of the country. However, many allege that China has also supplied arms to government fighters.

CHAPTER 3   Experiencing the Crisis in Darfur Firsthand

family behind, joined with unknown companions, and became a refugee in Egypt. She expresses little hope of seeing her family again.

FOREWORD

"History cannot give us a program for the future, but it can give us a fuller understanding of ourselves, and of our common humanity, so that we can better face the future."
—Robert Penn Warren,
American poet and novelist

The history of each nation is punctuated by momentous events that represent turning points for that nation, with an impact felt far beyond its borders. These events—displaying the full range of human capabilities, from violence, greed, and ignorance to heroism, courage, and strength—are nearly always complicated and multifaceted. Any student of history faces the challenge of grasping the many strands that constitute such world-changing events as wars, social movements, and environmental disasters. But understanding these significant historic events can be enhanced by exposure to a variety of perspectives, whether of people involved intimately or of ones observing from a distance of miles or years. Understanding can also be increased by learning about the controversies surrounding such events and exploring hot-button issues from multiple angles. Finally, true understanding of important historic events involves knowledge of the events' human impact—of the ways such events affected people in their everyday lives—all over the world.

Perspectives on Modern World History examines global historic events from the twentieth-century onward by presenting analysis and observation from numerous vantage points. Each volume offers high school, early college level, and general interest readers a thematically arranged anthology of previously published materials that address a major historical event, with an emphasis on international coverage. Each volume opens with background information on the event, then presents the controversies surrounding that event, and concludes with first-person narratives from people who lived through the event or were affected by it. By providing primary sources from the time of the event, as well as relevant commentary surrounding the event, this series can be used to inform debate, help develop critical thinking skills, increase global awareness, and enhance an understanding of international perspectives on history.

Material in each volume is selected from adiverse range of sources, including journals, magazines, newspapers, nonfiction books, personal narratives, speeches, congressional testimony, government documents, pamphlets, organization newsletters, and position papers Articles taken from these sources are carefully edited and introduced to provide context and background. Each volume of Perspectives on Modern World History includes an array of views on events of global significance. Much of the material comes from international sources and from U.S. sources that provide extensive international coverage.

Each volume in the Perspectives on Modern World History series also includes:

- A full-color **world map**, offering context and geographic perspective.
- An annotated **table of contents** that provides a brief summary of each essay in the volume.
- An **introduction** specific to the volume topic.
- For each viewpoint, a brief **introduction** that has notes about the author and source of the viewpoint, and that provides a summary of its main points.
- Full-color **charts**, **graphs**, **maps**, and other visual representations.

- Informational **sidebars** that explore the lives of key individuals, give background on historical events, or explain scientific or technical concepts.
- A **glossary** that defines key terms, as needed.
- A **chronology** of important dates preceding, during, and immediately following the event.
- A **bibliography** of additional books, periodicals, and Web sites for further research.
- A comprehensive **subject index** that offers access to people, places, and events cited in the text.

Perspectives on Modern World History is designed for a broad spectrum of readers who want to learn more about not only history but also current events, political science, government, international relations, and sociology—students doing research for class assignments or debates, teachers and faculty seeking to supplement course materials, and others wanting to improve their understanding of history. Each volume of Perspectives on Modern World History is designed to illuminate a complicated event, to spark debate, and to show the human perspective behind the world's most significant happenings of recent decades.

INTRODUCTION

In 2003, people in the United States began hearing news of fighting in a region in Africa known as Darfur. The region, in the west of the nation of Sudan, was little known to most, even though since the 1980s the U.S. had grown accustomed to bad news from the general area of Eastern and Central Africa where Sudan lies: famine, warfare, Islamic extremism, and even genocide in the nearby nation of Rwanda. Sudan had achieved some attention as a nation where Islamic extremists planning terrorist acts had taken refuge; indeed, in August 1998, U.S. warplanes had launched missile strikes at a pharmaceutical plant on the outskirts of Khartoum, Sudan's capital, partly due to Sudan's alleged ties to al Qaeda terrorists. But the news coming out of Darfur in 2003 was different. It described fighting between government-backed militia groups and local rebels, with Darfur's villagers caught in the crossfire, resulting in thousands of casualties and refugees.

Sudan is a nation with a complex history that stretches back for thousands of years. It contained civilizations on a par with, and in frequent contact with, the ancient Egypt of the pharaohs and the pyramids. At its geographical heart is the Upper Nile River; at its borders, the nation bleeds into the Sahara Desert to the north and west, touches the Red Sea in the east, and extends into relatively fertile grasslands in the south. Its population is equally diverse, being most commonly divided up into two sets of tribal groups. Arab Sudanese tribes dominate the north, the Nile Valley, and the capital, Khartoum, while native, or "black" African tribal groups populate the south and west. The majority of Sudanese practice Islam, although among the native African tribes there are also many Christians as well as those who maintain traditional animist customs and beliefs. For most of Sudan's history, these tribal groups, whether Arab or African, lived in relative autonomy, without any central government to control them. Among them was the tribe known as the Fur. From the 1300s to 1875, Fur leaders governed an independent Sultanate of Darfur in the west of the country. The tribe was incorporated into the solidifying nation of Sudan beginning in 1875, first under Egyptian rule and then under a self-proclaimed Islamic messiah, or Mahdi. When the Mahdi's government fell in 1899, British colonialists governed the territory. The British focused their attention on Khartoum and the Nile area, and Darfur remained poor and undeveloped after Sudan attained its independence in 1956.

Neglect of Darfur largely continued under Sudan's independent regimes. These regimes were dominated by Arabs, although leaders sometimes employed Darfurian agents to assist them in controlling the region. Problems in the area keep tensions high between Darfur and Khartoum. Among them was the expansion of the Sahara desert. This forced many Darfurians to abandon fields suffering from increasing "desertification" and therefore no longer fertile and to flee to already crowded inner areas. Another was the famine of 1984 and 1985. Many in the Western world associated the famine with the neighboring nation of Ethiopia, but it reached Sudan as well. Many Darfurians blamed the Khartoum government for its poor responses to these crises.

Other conflicts were more military in nature. Some involved intrigues with the nation of Libya, which used Darfur as a pawn in its attempt to expand its authority in the area. Others involved fighting in Chad, another neighbor, and even attempts by groups in southern Sudan to address their own grievances with Khartoum. Each of these conflicts resulted in a major reaction: The Sudanese government wanted to control Darfur and was ready to take increasingly drastic steps to do so. Darfurians themselves were constantly reminded of longstanding ethnic conflicts between Arab and native African tribes or, put another way, between a powerful center and an increasingly marginalized periphery. By the 1990s, Darfurians were involved in the increasingly assertive and rebellious Sudan People's Liberation Army while, for its part, the government tried to carve Darfur into three separate provinces in hopes of quelling any major threat. The first clashes between Arab and African groups took place in 1998 and 1999.

The clashes grew into a major rebellion in 2003, the year when meaningful news of the conflict leaked out to the world. By then two separate Darfurian organizations, the Sudan Liberation Army (SLA) and the Justice and Equality Movement (JEM) were ready to take decisive action against the government of Sudan. They charged Khartoum with favoring Arab interests over African ones and of general neglect of Darfur. The government's response to this 2003 rebellion resulted in what is known as the crisis in Darfur.

The Sudanese government's measures to quell the rebellion were brutal and drastic. Instead of using forces of the regular Sudanese military, the government sent into action militia groups, most notably the so-called Janjaweed, to terrorize and massacre Darfurian populations. Although Khartoum has denied any extensive connection with the militias, a general consensus of observers maintains that the government armed the Janjaweed and other militias, as well as provided intelligence and other forms of support. These militias killed civilians, raped women, and burned villages and fields in what some observers called an ethnic cleansing. The worst episodes of militia attacks took place in 2004. Many who were not killed fled or were simply uprooted. Refugee camps for these victims still existed years later, both in Darfur and across the border in Chad. Many refugees died of hunger, disease, or exposure. Estimates of those killed range from 10,000 (the government's claim) to as many as 300,000 or even 400,000 (the figures often used by humanitarian organizations).

The world's response to the growing crisis in Darfur was swift, perhaps especially because memories of the neglected genocide in Rwanda ten years before were still fresh. In January 2005, the United Nations passed a measure condemning the actions of the Sudanese government, although they stopped short of declaring the killings a genocide, or "race killing." The official position of the United States, however, was that the crisis in Darfur amounted to a genocide, a position first articulated in September 2004 by Secretary of State Colin Powell, when the fighting and killing were at their fiercest. The outcry in the United States, as well as in other nations, inspired the mounting of economic sanctions against Sudan, preventing outside investment and other forms of commerce with Khartoum. In 2007, the International Criminal Court took up the case, eventually accusing not only a Janjaweed leader but also Sudanese president Omar al-Bashir of genocide, crimes against humanity, and war crimes.

The responses to the crisis by people other than government officials were just as rapid and more varied, and they were helped along by a world increasingly interconnected via the Internet. By 2005, the crisis in Darfur was the subject of such projects as *The Darfur Diaries*, a collection of personal accounts of victims portrayed in a book, a documentary film, and a Web site. Even celebrities devoted their efforts to Darfur. Actor Mia Farrow has visited, photographed, and written on the subject of refugee camps. Actor Don Cheadle, who starred in a major Hollywood production dramatizing the Rwanda killings, cowrote a book on the subject. Actors such as George Clooney and Matt Damon, singers such as Bono and Fergie, and many other artists have also attempted to draw attention to the crisis. Human rights group Amnesty International even gathered many of the world's best-known musicians to contribute to *Instant Karma*, a 2007 album whose proceeds were devoted to Darfur. In 2008, many called for a boycott of that year's Summer Olympic Games in Beijing, China. China was accused of, at the very least, encouraging the violence in Sudan by providing Khartoum with much-needed outside capital and by searching the regions of the country, including Darfur, for natural resources to extract. Some accusers went even further, claiming that the Chinese were helping to arm the government's militias.

African nations, through the forum of the multinational African Union, took the lead in trying to bring peace to Darfur. Their efforts included a peacekeeping force sent to the region in 2005. That force was supplemented by a larger, and to some minds more effective, United Nations peacekeeping force in 2007. This combined force—which by the end of 2009 was declaring the large-scale fighting in Darfur over—was known as the United Nations African Union Mission in Sudan, or UNAMID. The African Union has also provided the framework by which peace terms could be negotiated between the Sudanese government and the rebel groups. The negotiations, which began in 2006 in Abuja, Nigeria, proceeded haltingly. By the end of 2009, however, the various factions of the two major rebel organizations, the SLA and the JEM, had entered into agreements with Khartoum to stop large-scale warfare in Darfur.

The year 2010 finds Sudan in an uneasy state of peace, although fighting continues to flare up from time to time between the Sudanese government and Darfurian rebels. The nation is ironically enjoying a prolonged economic boom based primarily on the export of oil and other resources, exports that go to nations that, like China, do not maintain economic sanctions against Sudan. In Darfur itself, meanwhile, and across the border in Chad, refugee camps are still full, and refugees are afraid to go home.

World Map

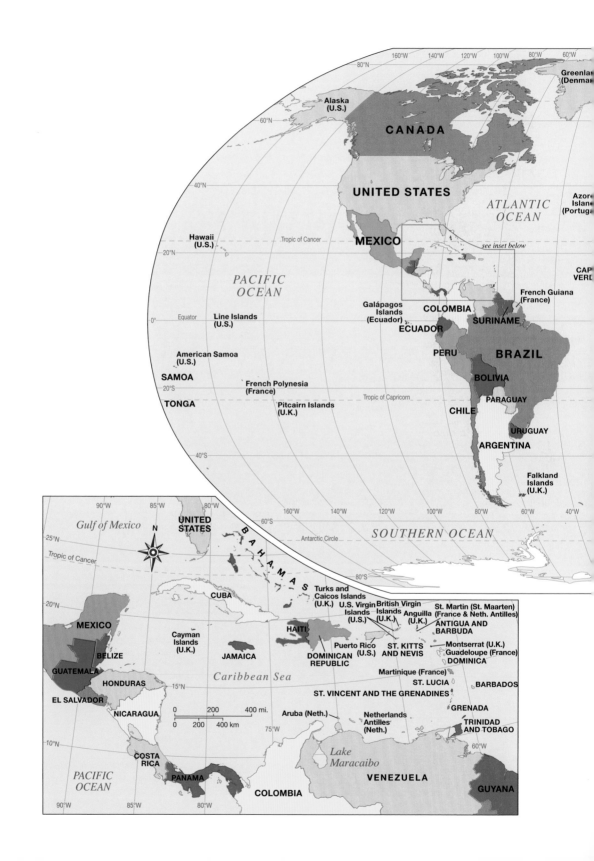

160°W   140°W   120°W   100°W   80°W   60°W

80°N

Greenland
(Denmar

Alaska
(U.S.)

60°N

CANADA

40°N

UNITED STATES

*ATLANTIC
OCEAN*

Azore
Island
(Portuga

Hawaii
(U.S.)

Tropic of Cancer

MEXICO

see inset below

CAP
VERDE

20°N

*PACIFIC
OCEAN*

Galápagos
Islands
(Ecuador)

COLOMBIA

French Guiana
(France)

Line Islands
(U.S.)

Equator   0°

ECUADOR

SURINAME

American Samoa
(U.S.)

PERU

BRAZIL

SAMOA

French Polynesia
(France)

BOLIVIA

20°S

TONGA

Pitcairn Islands
(U.K.)

Tropic of Capricorn

PARAGUAY

CHILE

URUGUAY

ARGENTINA

40°S

Falkland
Islands
(U.K.)

160°W   140°W   120°W   100°W   80°W   60°W   40°W

60°S

Antarctic Circle

SOUTHERN OCEAN

80°S

90°W   85°W   80°W

Gulf of Mexico   **UNITED
STATES**   N

25°N

Tropic of Cancer

B
A
H
A
M
A
S

Turks and
Caicos Islands
(U.K.)

U.S. Virgin British Virgin
Islands   Islands Anguilla
(U.S.)   (U.K.)   (U.K.)

St. Martin (St. Maarten)
(France & Neth. Antilles)
**ANTIGUA AND
BARBUDA**

CUBA

20°N

MEXICO

Cayman
Islands
(U.K.)

HAITI

Puerto Rico
(U.S.)

**ST. KITTS
AND NEVIS**

Montserrat (U.K.)
Guadeloupe (France)
DOMINICA

BELIZE

JAMAICA

**DOMINICAN
REPUBLIC**

Martinique (France)

GUATEMALA

Caribbean Sea

ST. LUCIA   **BARBADOS**

HONDURAS

15°N

ST. VINCENT AND THE GRENADINES

EL SALVADOR

NICARAGUA

0   200   400 mi.

0   200   400 km

75°W

Aruba (Neth.)

Netherlands
Antilles
(Neth.)

GRENADA

**TRINIDAD
AND TOBAGO**

60°W

10°N

**COSTA
RICA**

*Lake
Maracaibo*

*PACIFIC
OCEAN*

PANAMA

VENEZUELA

GUYANA

90°W   85°W   80°W

COLOMBIA

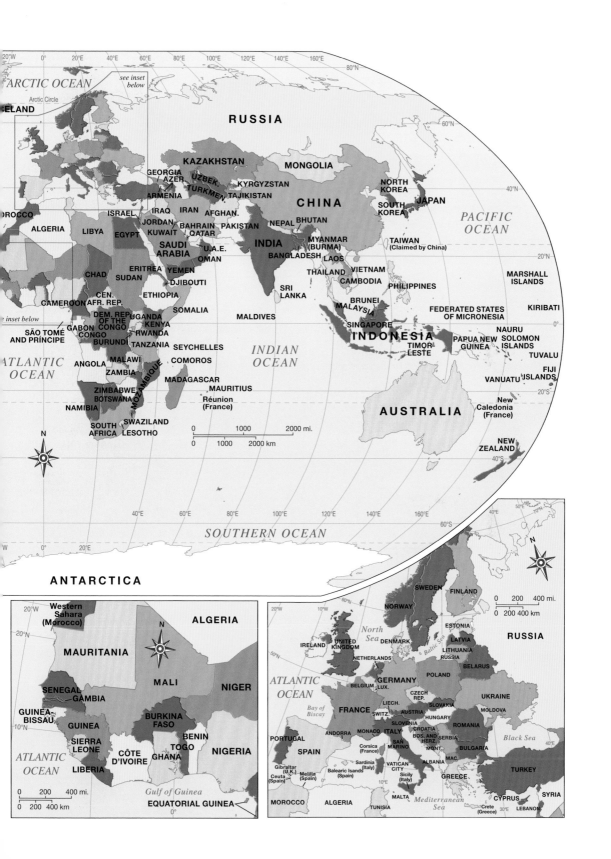

CHAPTER 1

Historical Background on the Crisis in Darfur

Darfur's History of Diversity, Colonialism, and Ethnic Conflict

New Internationalist

The following is a summary of Darfur's history compiled by an activist organization called the New Internationalist Workers Cooperative. It examines how a network of local African tribal groups was integrated with Arab settlers over a number of years and how, over the last two centuries, both Africans and Arabs lived under colonial overlords such as the Ottoman and British empires. Its focus, however, is on Darfur's more recent history.

The British granted independence to the nation of Sudan, which includes the region of Darfur, in 1956. They left most of the power in the hands of "northern Arab elites," the authors of the selection note. Sudan's subsequent history has been marked by interference from foreign powers in addition to internal conflicts and a broad famine that struck the region in the 1980s. In 1989, General Omar al-Bashir took power, turning Sudan into a staging area for Islamic fundamentalist terrorists.

Photo on previous page: The village of Terbeba in Darfur was one of several damaged and destroyed by the pro-Sudanese government Janjaweed militia. (**Julie Flint/AFP/ Getty Images.**)

SOURCE. "Darfur—A History," *New Internationalist*, June 2007. Copyright © 2007 New Internationalist Magazine. Reproduced by permission.

The authors note that General al-Bashir's role has continued to inflame ethnic and tribal conflicts, notably in the southern region of Darfur.

Darfur's people are a complex mosaic of between 40 and 90 ethnic groups, some of 'African' origin (mostly settled farmers), some Arabs. All Darfurians are Muslim. The Arabs began arriving in the 14th century and established themselves as mainly nomadic cattle and camel herders. Peaceful coexistence has been the norm, with inevitable disputes over resources between fixed and migratory communities resolved through the mediation of local leaders. For much of its history, the division between 'Arab' and 'African' has been blurred at best, with so much intermarriage that all Darfurians can claim mixed ancestry. Identities have been defined in different ways at different times, based on race, speech, appearance or way of life.

An Independent Sultanate

At the heart of Darfur is an extinct volcano in a mountainous area called Jebel Marra. Around it the land is famously fertile, and it was here that the earliest known inhabitants of Darfur lived—the Daju. Very little is known about them. The recorded history of Darfur begins in the 14th century, when the Daju dynasty was superseded by the Tunjur, who brought Islam to the region.

Darfur existed as an independent state for several hundred years. In the mid-17th century, the Keyra Fur Sultanate was established, and Darfur prospered.

In its heyday in the 17th and 18th centuries the Fur Sultanate's geographical location made it a thriving commercial hub, trading with the Mediterranean in slaves, ivory and ostrich feathers, raiding its neighbours and fighting wars of conquest in the surrounding region.

Darfur Under Siege

In the mid-19th century, Darfur's sultan was defeated by notorious slave trader Zubayr Rahma, who was in turn subjugated by the Ottoman Empire. At the time, this included Egypt and what is now northern Sudan. The collapse of the Keyra dynasty plunged Darfur into lawlessness. Roaming bandits and local armies preyed on vulnerable communities, and Islamic 'Mahdist' forces [led by a "Mahdi", or Messiah figure in Shia Islam] fighting British colonial control of the region sought to incorporate Darfur into a much larger Islamic republic. A period of almost constant war followed, until 1899 when the Egyptians—now under British rule—recognized Ali Dinar, grandson of one of the Keyra sultans, as Sultan of Darfur. This marked a *de facto* [actual, but not by law] return to independence, and Darfur lived in peace for a few years.

Colonial 'Benign Neglect'

Ali Dinar refused to submit to the wishes of either the French or the British, who were busy building their empires around his territory. Diplomatic friction turned into open warfare. Ali Dinar defied the British forces for six months, but was ambushed and killed, along with his two sons, in November 1916. In January 1917 Darfur was absorbed into the British Empire and became part of Sudan, making this the largest country in Africa.

> Darfur has been treated as an unimportant backwater, a pawn in power games, by its successive rulers.

The only aim of Darfur's new colonial rulers was to keep the peace. Entirely uninterested in the region's development (or lack thereof), no investment was forthcoming. In stark contrast to the north of Sudan, by 1935 Darfur had only four schools, no maternity clinic, no railways or major roads outside the largest towns. Darfur has been treated as an unimportant backwater, a pawn in power games, by its successive rulers ever since.

Independence Brings War

The British reluctantly but peacefully granted Sudan independence in 1956. The colonialists had kept North and South Sudan separate, developing the fertile lands around the Nile Valley in the North, whilst neglecting the South, East and Darfur to the west. They handed over political power directly to a minority of northern Arab élites who, in various groupings, have been in power ever since. This caused the South to mutiny in 1955, starting

The Mahdi

One of the more dramatic and colorful episodes in Sudan's history took place in the 1880s and 1890s. Then, much of the country was swept by a wave of serious Islamic devotion when large armies formed to follow a figure who called himself the Mahdi.

In Islamic history, the Mahdi is considered to be a figure of redemption. Ancient teachings suggest that this redeemer would appear to help usher in and preside over an age of justice, peace, and devotion. Belief in the Mahdi is part of the Shia branch of the Islamic religion but is seen less often among Sunni Muslims, who are the great majority of the religion's followers. Mahdism can also be found among many Sufi orders. Sufi Muslims practice a mystical form of the faith.

The Mahdi who emerged in Sudan in the 1880s was such a Sufi. His given name was Muhammad Ahmad (1844–1885), and he was born into a Northern

Sudanese Arab clan that claimed to be descended from Muhammad, the original prophet and founder of Islam. From an early age he devoted his life to religious study and meditation and rose to be the leader, or sheikh, of one of Sudan's largest Sufi orders. In 1881, he proclaimed that he was the Mahdi. While other Sudanese Islamic leaders rejected the claim, he found wide popularity among ordinary people. For decades, many Sudanese had lived under the harsh rule of Egyptians generally loyal to the Turkish Empire based in faraway Istanbul and, from 1873, British general Charles Gordon acting as an agent of Egypt. The Mahdi promised not only religious redemption but a movement based in native Sudanese customs and traditions which would ensure the power of Sudanese Arabs.

When the Sudanese government tried to silence him in 1881, the Mahdi declared jihad, one definition of which

the first North-South war. It lasted until 1972 when peace was signed under President [Gaafar] Nimeiry. But the Government continually flouted the peace agreement. This, combined with its shift towards imposing radical political Islam on an unwilling people, and the discovery of oil, reignited conflict in the South in 1983.

Darfur, meanwhile, became embroiled in the various conflicts raging around it: not just internal wars by the centre over its marginalized populations—many of

is to conduct warfare for the faith. In a march through Sudan's south he built up an army of followers, or "Ansar." By 1883, this force numbered some 40,000 troops, far larger than any Egyptian force that could be mustered against it. The Mahdi's rebellion spread quickly. By 1884 he controlled most of western and southern Sudan, including the formerly troublesome region of Darfur.

British general Gordon had left Khartoum, Sudan's capital, in 1880, but he returned in 1884 to help Egyptian troops evacuate to the north. The Mahdi's troops quickly surrounded Khartoum, forcing Gordon and his supporters to endure a long siege. The siege finally broke in January 1885. Gordon was killed in the fighting, and his head later presented to the Mahdi. With the fall of Khartoum, little could prevent the Ansar from completing its conquest of the rest of the country.

The Mahdi's government tried to instill Islamic unity and minimize the nation's long history of tribal and ethnic conflict. The Mahdi enforced a fairly strict version of Sharia, or Islamic law, and required believers to acknowledge him in their daily prayers as the representative of the Prophet. Having prepared for the eventuality, the Mahdi even ensured that his government would hold despite his death from typhus in mid-1885. His chief successor, who called himself "Khalifa" or "successor," was finally defeated by a returning, and now stronger, British force in 1899. From that year until 1956, Sudan remained under joint British-Egyptian control. To the modern day, a number of Sudanese continue to respect the Mahdi as the founder of Sudanese nationalism.

the soldiers who fought for the Government against the South were Darfurian recruits—but also regional struggles. The use of Darfur by Libya's Colonel [Muammar] Qadafhi as a military base for his Islamist wars in Chad promoted Arab supremacism, inflamed ethnic tensions, flooded the region with weaponry and sparked the Arab-Fur war (1987–89), in which thousands were killed and hundreds of Fur villages burned. The people's suffering was exacerbated by a devastating famine in the mid-1980s, during which the Government abandoned Darfurians to their fate.

> "The government used ethnic militias to fight as proxy forces for them."

Al-Bashir Seizes Power

In 1989 the National Islamic Front (NIF), led by General Omar al-Bashir, seized power in Sudan from the democratically elected government of Sadiq al Mahdi, in a bloodless coup. The NIF revoked the constitution, banned opposition parties, unravelled steps towards peace and instead proclaimed *jihad* [a war of faith] against the non-Muslim South, regularly using ethnic militias to do the fighting. Although depending on Muslim Darfur for political support, the NIF's programme of 'Arabization' further marginalized the region's 'African' population.

The regime harboured several Islamic fundamentalist organizations, including providing a home for Osama bin Laden from 1991 until 1996, when the US forced his expulsion. Sudan was implicated in the June 1995 assassination attempt on Egyptian President [Hosni] Mubarak. Its support for terrorists and increasing international isolation culminated in a US cruise-missile attack on a Sudanese pharmaceutical factory in 1998, following terrorist bombings of the US embassies in Nairobi and Dar es Salaam.

The first north–south war in Sudan began in 1955 and continued until 1972, when a peace agreement was signed under former president Gaafar Nimeiry. **(AP Photo/ Abdel Raouf.)**

The Janjaweed: 'Counterinsurgency on the Cheap'

Janjaweed fighters, with their philosophy of violent Arab supremacism, were first active in Darfur in the Arab-Fur war in the late 1980s. Recruited mainly from Arab nomadic tribes, demobilized soldiers and criminal elements, the word *janjaweed* means 'hordes' or 'ruffians', but also sounds like 'devil on horseback' in Arabic. The ruthlessly opportunistic Sudanese Government first armed, trained and deployed them against the Massalit people of Darfur in 1996–98. This was an established strategy by which the Government used ethnic militias to fight as proxy forces for them. It allowed the Government to fight local wars cheaply, and also to deny it was behind the conflict, despite overwhelming evidence to the contrary.

The Comprehensive Peace Agreement

When President George W. Bush came to power in 2000, US policy shifted from isolationism to engagement with Sudan. After 11 September 2001 Bashir 'fell into line', started to co-operate with the US in their 'war on terror' and a peace process began in earnest in the South. After years of painstaking negotiations, and under substantial pressure from the US, in January 2005 a Comprehensive Peace Agreement (CPA) was signed between the Government and the Sudan People's Liberation Movement/Army (SPLM/A), ending 21 years of bloody war which killed two million people, displaced another four million and razed southern Sudan to the ground.

A surprisingly favourable deal for the South, the CPA included a power-sharing agreement leading up to a referendum on independence for the South in 2011, a 50-50 share of the profits from its lucrative oilfields, national elections in 2009 and 10,000 UN peacekeepers to oversee the agreement's implementation. But the 'comprehensive' deal completely ignored Darfur, catalyzing the conflict that is currently engulfing the region.

The Rebels Attack

Rebellion had been brewing in marginalized, poverty-stricken Darfur for years. After decades in the political wilderness, being left out of the peace negotiations was the final straw. Inspired by the SPLA's success, rebel attacks against Government targets became increasingly frequent as two main rebel groups emerged—the Sudan Liberation Army (SLA) and the Justice and Equality Movement (JEM). By early 2003 they had formed an alliance. Attacks on garrisons, and a joint attack in April on an airbase that reduced several Government planes and helicopters to ashes, were causing serious damage and running rings around the Sudanese army.

Facing the prospect of its control over the entire country unravelling, in 2003 the Government decided to counterattack. Manipulating ethnic tensions that had flared up in Darfur around access to increasingly scarce land and water resources, they unleashed the Janjaweed to attack communities they claimed had links to the rebels.

The Crisis in Darfur Is Another Episode in Sudan's History of Conflicts

Robert O. Collins

> Formerly part of the British Empire, the nation of Sudan became independent in 1956. According to scholar Robert O. Collins, the author of the following selection, Sudan's history since then has featured the sorts of ethnic conflict and violence that flared up once again in Darfur in 2003. Collins notes how Sudanese of Arab background, who are often at the center of power in Khartoum, the nation's capital, have held African Sudanese from the nation's south, east, and west in disdain, oppressing them even to the level of slavetrading. In response, African Sudanese—who hail from a variety of regional, tribal, and even religious backgrounds—have sought to defend themselves. Through two civil wars since 1955, these African Sudanese

SOURCE. Robert O. Collins, *Encyclopedia of Genocide and Crimes Against Humanity*. Belmont, CA: Gale, 2005. Copyright © 2005 by Gale Publishing. Reproduced by permission of Gale, a part of Cengage Learning.

have been marginalized, targeted, and displaced. Robert O. Collins was a professor of African history at the University of California, Santa Barbara.

The declaration of an independent Sudan on January 1, 1956, and the departure of British officials did not result in any resurgence of slavery, which had been contained but not completely eliminated. The peaceful transfer of power, however, was marred by the mutiny of the Equatorial Corps of the Sudan Defense Force in the southern Sudan. The mutiny was suppressed, but it ignited the longest civil war in any country in the twentieth century, one that has continued into the twenty-first century. From its beginnings in 1955 the southern insurgency has became a symbol of the antagonism created by the nineteenth-century reality of slavery and the twentieth-century perceptions of racism among Arabs from the north who regarded the southern Sudanese as slaves (*'abid*) or property (*malkiyya*). Reports issued by the United Nations (UN) and in the international media of vulnerable African southern Sudanese being forced into involuntary servitude have been vehemently denied by the Sudanese government, but the government's incompetence in governing its vast hinterland and its ideology, combined with famine, war, and racism, have provided the opportunity for the revival of customary practices of slavery, euphemistically referred to as abductions, and its trade. In the violence of civil war, human rights have been ignored and innocent African civilians slaughtered by the thousands. Although the southern Sudan is the conspicuous scene of this terrible conflict, no government of the Sudan at Khartoum has

> No government of the Sudan at Khartoum has effectively governed the marginalized Sudanese people on the periphery in the south, west, or east.

effectively governed the marginalized Sudanese people on the periphery in the south, west, or east.

Independent Sudan: Since 1956

So long as Sudanese government officials cannot control the country, whatever may be their ideologies, political persuasion, or religious beliefs regarding human relationships, slavery, and the indiscriminate slaughter associated with the seizure of slaves will continue in the Sudan. The northern Sudanese have done little to disguise their contempt for the African Sudanese from the non-Arab regions because of their color, culture, and religion. In the half-century of independence in the Sudan, the ill-defined concept of race has complicated the confusion of identity in the Sudan and reinforced historic perceptions of inferiority that may no longer be legal, yet confirm convictions of superiority that are more pervasive and powerful than the law. The persistence of this doleful inheritance has been a central cause of a rationale justifying, the killing fields in the southern Sudan.

The First Civil War: 1955 to 1972

The southern disturbances of August 1955 marked the beginning of resistance by the African Sudanese practicing traditional religions or Christianity against the government in Khartoum, dominated by the northern Arab, Muslim Sudanese. In 1964 Christian missionaries were expelled from the Sudan. They had been the teachers of the small southern Sudanese elite who soon organized rudimentary associations to mobilize political dissent and to create the African, non-Muslim southern guerrilla forces, known as *Anya Nya* (snake venom). After eighteen years of fighting President Ja'Far Numayri, the *Anya Nya* signed an agreement at Addis Ababa in 1972 that conferred on the southern provinces a modest degree of autonomy which brought an end to the fighting but not the political turmoil between the northern and

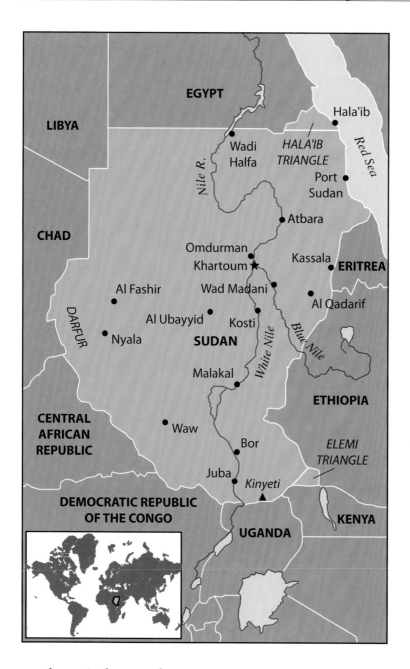

southern Sudan. Within ten years Numayri unilaterally abrogated the Addis Ababa Accords in a futile attempt to secure the support of the Islamists, Muslim fundamentalists in the Sudan, who sought to impose Islam and its laws (*Shari'a*) on non-Muslim African Sudanese. The southern Sudanese resumed their fighting in 1983, led by Colonel John Garang, who reorganized former guerrilla *Anya Nya* fighters into the Sudan People's Liberation Movement/Army (SPLM/SPLA).

The First Civil War, 1955 through 1972, ended with a litany of brutality and terrorism in remote places where accountability was of little concern and the media absent. The fighting was unremitting for the civilians and debilitating for the army of the Sudan. The conflict displaced thousands of southern Sudanese, resulting in a massive number of refugees. It created a coterie of exiled southern elite. It destroyed the fragile infrastructure left by the British. It produced Christian martyrs. It convinced many southern Sudanese that there could be no compromise with the northern Sudanese.

Second Civil War: Since 1983

By 1984 Garang had consolidated the SPLM/A and forced the termination of the exploration for oil and the construction of the Jonglei Canal to supply additional water for irrigation in the northern Sudan and Egypt. Meanwhile, the SPLA, supplemented by substantial defections from the security forces, had occupied extensive areas in the rural south and driven the Sudan army onto the defensive in the major towns of Juba, Wau, and Malakal. To add to the disastrous consequences produced by war, African drought and the decision by the Sudan government in 1984 to distribute automatic weapons to the Baggara tribesmen of Darfur and Kordofan, members of the Arab militia or *murahileen*, combined to escalate war-related deaths of the southern Sudanese into the hundreds of thousands. The great African drought of the 1980s devastated the plains of the Sahil from Senegal across Africa through Darfur, Kordofan, and into southern Sudan. Here the population had been increasing more rapidly than the production of food and livestock. Customary exchange in times of hardship collapsed. Crops failed to germinate without water, and the cattle died without grass. During the winter of 1984 and 1985 tens of thousands of southern Sudanese, Nilotes, and Equatorians began to flee into southern towns and then to the north and to Ethiopia seeking food. By January 1987 hundreds of thousands of southern Sudanese were dead or in flight to the anonymity of towns and the camps for the displaced from Kordofan to Khartoum and from the Bahr al-Ghazal to Ethiopia to avoid death from starvation and war, with disease often accompanying starvation.

In 1984 Numayri's Minister of Defense, General Suwar al-Dhahab, equipped the Arab militia with automatic weapons and unleashed these *murahileen* into the southern Sudan in a desperate attempt to stem the spread of the rebellion among the Dinka who were allied with Garang, a Dinka from Bor. The raiders were mostly young Rizayqat and Messiriya Baggara tribes-men who, imbued with the folklore of their forefathers, raided the Dinka for cattle, pastures, and *'abid* (slaves), and felt they had a license to kill in order to replenish their own herds decimated by drought. With their superiority over a traditional enemy guaranteed by the AK-47, the tenuous equilibrium that had existed for more than a half-century on the Baggara-Dinka frontier dissolved into a *razzia* [raid] of indiscriminate plunder and wanton killing. A somnolent village would be surrounded before dawn and attacked at first light. The women, children, and teenage males that had not escaped were collected with the cattle. The men were indiscriminately killed, often accompanied by mutilation, and the village and cultivations were then methodically destroyed and the Dinka cattle, women, and children divided among the Baggara to serve or to be sold.

By 1987 the SPLA had established its military presence in the Bahr al-Ghazal, inflicting heavy casualties on the Baggara militia and the officers and men of the army, the Sudan People's Armed Forces (SPAF). On the night of March 27, 1987, more than a thousand Dinka were immolated and slaughtered at Ed Diein in southern Darfur in a vengeful race riot. In November the SPLA captured Kurmuk, producing a hysteria in Khartoum that culminated in the successful coup d'état of Umar Hasan Ahmad al-Bashir on June 30, 1989. He installed the first theocratic Islamist government in the Sudan. His supporters, the National Islamic Front (NIF), were more determined than ever to defeat the southern Sudanese insurgents in order to impose Islam and Arab culture on the Africans of the southern Sudan.

Islamist Government of the Sudan: Since 1989

Unlike many coups d'état that are motivated by discontent, the officers who seized control of the Sudan government on June 30th were determined to construct a new Sudan defined by Islam, with the laws of the Q'uran (*Shari'a*) interpreted and regulated by the doctrines of the National Islamic Front (NIF) and promulgated by the Revolutionary Government of National Salvation led by Umar al-Bashir. To be Sudanese was to conform to the rigid ideology of the Islamists. Whoever refused to conform to its creed would be excluded for not being Sudanese. To produce the new Sudan, the Islamists introduced a complete ideology that affected all aspects of life in the Sudan. It was an attempt to indoctrinate, shape, and thereby control the Sudanese to produce a homogeneous Islamic society even if it required the destruction of the *kafirin*, unbelieving Africans in the southern Sudan, by jihad (holy war). By 1991 the *Shari'a* had been embodied in the Sudan penal code; in 1992 Islamic legal traditions were employed to justify the jihad against apostates and heathens; after 1993 Islamic principles were invoked as the guide for all agencies of government, civilian and military. The creation of the new Sudan as a monolithic and homogeneous society reduced the non-Muslim African Sudanese before the law and in society to less than equal status. The legal and religious definition of non-Muslim Sudanese Africans as second-class citizens provided welcome relief, if not justification by the Islamists in Khartoum to carry on total war with greater intensity. During the decade of drought and the *razzia* (1983–1993) more than 1 million southern Sudanese died and another 4 million became refugees in foreign countries, or internally displaced within the Sudan.

Having little confidence in the SPAF to pursue a jihad aggressively, the NIF-controlled government introduced universal conscription to create the People's Defense Forces (PDF) composed of raw recruits and government-supported militias. In 1990 the air force began indiscriminate aerial bombing of civilians in the southern Sudan; its only targets were villages, cattle, churches, schools, and hospitals. An estimated eleven thousand Sudanese were either killed or wounded. The offensive was symbolic of more demonstrable efforts by the SPAF, supported by the PDF, to eliminate the presence of the SPLA by premeditated ethnic cleansing. Between 1990 and 2000 the jihad in the Nuba Mountains had killed more than an estimated 100,000 and resettled another 170,000 Nuba in so-called peace villages on the Sahilean plains of Kordofan where they labored in fields and towns for northern Sudanese entrepreneurs.

During the same decade, military offensives by the SPAF and the *razzia* of the Baggara *murahileen* and the Dinka militia of Kerubino Kwanjin Bol, who had defected from the SPLA to join the government forces, resulted in the death of another estimated 200,000 Dinka and Nuer in the Bahr al-Ghazal by killing and famine. Others were displaced by the hundreds of thousands. During the drought of 1993 and 1994 the Sudan government deliberately intervened in the distribution of

This Darfur rebel claims both African and Arab ancestry. Unclear notions of race complicated the ethnic tensions of the conflict. (AP Photo/ **Alfred de Montesquiou.**)

humanitarian food aid by Operation Lifeline, a Western organization. The Sudan effectively utilized famine as a weapon of war to depopulate large areas of the Bahr al-Ghazal by starvation, forcing its inhabitants to become internally displaced persons (IDP).

In the Upper Nile in 1991 the SPLA commanders Riak Machar, Lam Akol, and Gordon Kong Cuol formed a rival South Sudan Independence Movement/Army (SSIM/A) to overthrow Garang. The SSIM/A was dominated by the Nuer. In a formal alliance with the Sudan government, they received large numbers of automatic weapons that they promptly used to kill many thousand of their traditional Dinka enemies who were supporters of the SPLA and their kinsman, Garang. The ensuing local Nilotic civil war within the larger Sudan civil war killed more southerners than the SPAF. The southern Sudanese casualties from 1991 to 2000 are estimated at approximately 250,000, and an equal number of southerners were displaced. In Equatoria, the heartland of the SPLA, the fighting intensified throughout the decade as the SPAF sought to capitalize on the bitter feud within the SPLA to recapture strategic towns they had previously lost. During this same tragic decade in Equatoria war-related deaths averaged ten thousand per year.

Although oil had been discovered on the northern borders of the southern Sudan in 1976, the renewal of the civil war in 1983 delayed its export by pipeline to Port Sudan until August 1999. At this time further exploration demonstrated that large Sudanese oil reserves were located in the sudd and surrounding grassland plains of the Upper Nile and Bahr al-Ghazal. These oil-rich regions could obviously not be exploited if controlled by southern insurgents, whether the militias of southern warlords or the SPLA that had frustrated the development of Sudanese oil for twenty years. In order to secure the oil fields, the government launched military offensives to clear the land of southern Sudanese by killing its inhabitants and their cattle and forcing the survivors to seek refuge in the southern Bahr al-Ghazal as internally displaced persons. The government then had at its disposal millions of dollars from oil revenues. Over half of this money was used to purchase sophisticated weapons and the especially feared helicopter gun ships, which are more effective at driving people off the land than the indiscriminate high-level bombing of the past. Better equipped, the regular army, the PDF, and the southern Sudanese militias were initially successful in their campaigns of ethnic cleansing to secure the flat pasture lands of the western Upper Nile and eastern Bahr al-Ghazal. The war-related deaths of the southern Sudanese continued to grow. . . .

The Question of Genocide

After a half-century of civil war punctuated by a decade of peace (1972–1983) and infrequent ceasefires during which a host of international mediators have sought to broker a peace between the Sudan government and the SPLM/A, the question of genocide on the part of the Sudan government was first raised by the international non-governmental organizations (NGOs) working in the Sudan, and then discussed at the UN and in the international media. After 1989 the determination of the Islamist government of Umar al-Bashir to defeat the southern insurgents and impose by jihad Islam, Arabization, and the Shari'a throughout the southern Sudan leaves little doubt that the government in Khartoum actively participated or quietly condoned the death by famine or slaughter of hundreds of thousands of civilian African Sudanese. There are numerous definitions of genocide, but the standard definition is contained in the 1948 UN Convention on the Prevention and Punishment of the Crime of Genocide. Genocide means the intent to destroy, in whole or part, any national, ethic, racial, or religious group by killing, bodily harm, preventing birth, or transferring children from that group to another one.

Although there is no evidence that the Sudan government officially adopted a policy to eliminate any particular ethnic group in the southern Sudan or the southern Sudanese as a whole, their policies involved the indiscriminate aerial bombing of civilians and their installations, the withholding of humanitarian aid to cause death by starvation, and silent indifference to the activities by government-supported militias to loot, kidnap, and enslave. The Islamist government has worked assiduously to deny these charges by defending its actions as a necessary military response to defeat the southern Sudanese insurgents, the SPLA, preserve the unity of the Sudan, and incorporate the African Sudanese into an Islamic, Arab Sudan. Under international pressure the government of Umar al-Bashir has sought to dispel the accusations of genocide by greater cooperation with the West and a willingness to discuss peace with the SPLA. Without peace in the Sudan there is no prospect of resolving whether the massive loss of southern Sudanese lives was, in fact, a deliberate policy of genocide by the government of the Sudan.

The Human Toll of the Darfur Fighting Is Uncertain

Associated Press

In the following selection, journalists examine the problem of accurately counting the number of Darfurians who have died or been displaced as a result of the fighting that began in 2003. Writing in 2006, when the violence seemed to be escalating, the authors report that the estimates of the death toll from outside observers such as United Nations groups ranged from 200,000 to 400,000 people. Meanwhile Sudan's government claimed that the number of dead was much lower. The article explains that many problems contributed to the uncertainty and confusion about the estimates. Few aid organizations or other observers had access to the entire Darfur region, and the refugee camps that many of the displaced lived in were temporary, sometimes even springing up in the neighboring country of Chad. Many deaths, in addition, were due to hunger or exacerbated by the violent attacks. A target of the criticisms

SOURCE. "Debate Over Darfur Death Toll Intensifies," *USA Today*, November 29, 2006. Copyright © 2007 The Associated Press. All rights reserved. Reprinted with permission of the Associated Press.

from many figures quoted in the selection was a new organization known as the United Nations Human Rights Council, which some officials felt did little to acknowledge the Sudan government's role in the crisis.

As violence in Darfur escalates, a debate is growing over how many people have died in what officials call the world's worst humanitarian crisis. A U.N. [United Nations] agency's survey cites at least 200,000 deaths, but other studies say the death toll could be closer to 400,000 or more.

Sudan's government, however, contends the deaths are only a tiny fraction of that.

The dispute occurs in part because, ever since fighting began in early 2003, humanitarian workers have had only limited and perilous access to Darfur, a sprawling, arid region of western Sudan nearly the size of Texas.

> "Ever since fighting began in early 2003, humanitarian workers have had only limited and perilous access to Darfur.

Both violence and government restrictions have kept aid groups and researchers away. Right now, for example, violence makes nearly 40% of the population inaccessible to aid workers, said Ramesh Rajasingham, the head of the U.N. Office for Coordination of Humanitarian Affairs in Sudan.

"To this day, we don't really have our eyes on the ground. We work with projections," Rajasingham said in a recent interview.

Overall, the U.N. says 4 million people in Darfur are currently in desperate need of aid—nearly two-thirds of the estimated Darfur population of 6.5 million. An estimated 2.5 million live in refugee camps in Darfur and neighboring Chad, while others inhabit remote villages, the U.N. says.

Council Vote Criticized

Top U.N. officials said Wednesday [November 29, 2006] that the U.N. Human Rights Council has ignored the Sudanese government's role in atrocities being committed in Darfur, and called on it to ignore regional and other loyalties and stand up to regimes that violate human rights.

The comments came one day after the 47-nation body rejected an attempt to hold the Sudanese government responsible for halting the brutal attacks on civilians in Darfur.

"It's very strange that (the council) was quiet on Darfur for such a long time," Jan Egeland, the U.N. undersecretary-general for humanitarian affairs, told reporters in Geneva. "They obviously do not meet the raped women and the abused civilians. They do not see the true picture."

U.N. human rights chief Louise Arbour criticized nations that are "in denial about Darfur."

The rights council, which in its six months of existence has only criticized Israel, rejected by a vote of 22-20 a resolution from the European Union and Canada calling on the Sudanese government to prosecute those responsible for killing, raping and injuring civilians in Darfur.

Instead, it accepted a resolution from African countries and supported by Muslim nations that called on all parties in the conflict to end human rights violations. The council also praised Sudan's government for cooperating with a U.N.-appointed rights expert.

Tuesday's vote at the council, which replaced the widely discredited Human Rights Commission in June, followed months of negotiations between Western countries and the so-called African Group led by Algeria on what approach to take toward Darfur. The United Nations has called Darfur the world's worst humanitarian disaster.

The council's resolution does not criticize President Omar al-Bashir's government, which has been accused

of unleashing brutal militiamen known as janjaweed in fighting Darfur rebels. The janjaweed are alleged to have destroyed hundreds of villages, killing the inhabitants, raping women and stealing livestock.

A Darfur survivor stands near what he believes is a mass grave of his friends and fellow villagers. (AP Photo/ Nasser Nasser.)

Khartoum's delegate to the council, Ibrahim Mirghani Ibrahim, said the situation in Darfur had improved. Jordan's ambassador, Mousa Burayzat, blamed the international media for distorting the situation.

But Arbour, the U.N. human rights chief, told the council Wednesday that "attacks on villages, killing of civilians, rape and the forced displacement of tens of thousands of civilians go on unabated."

"The government of Sudan and militias aligned with them, and some still actively supported by them, continue to be responsible for the most serious violations of international human rights and humanitarian law," she said.

U.S. Ambassador John Bolton said the vote on the Darfur resolutions was "another disappointment . . . another example of the poor performance of the Human Rights Council, another reason why those who advocated going ahead with this council will have a heavy burden to bear."

> A team from the World Health Organization estimated that 10,000 of these refugees died each month between the end of 2003 and October 2004.

Over a third of the nations that sit on the council are members of the 57-nation Organization of the Islamic Conference. The Islamic Conference nations—with the support of China, Russia, India, Cuba and the African nations—have come to dominate the council's proceedings.

[UN Secretary-General Kofi] Annan said the council should "build coalitions based on principle" and not divide itself along factional lines.

He urged the council to give "human rights a priority on a par with that accorded to peace and security and to development," saying that will happen only if the council is determined "to uphold human rights worldwide."

"Do not let yourselves be split along the fault line between north and south, between developed and developing countries," he said. "Only by showing such courage and rigor can you avoid disappointing the many people around the world who look to the U.N. for support in their struggle for human rights, and driving them to turn elsewhere."

Observers Estimate Death Increase

On deaths, the last official, independent mortality survey for Darfur was published in March 2005. Based on data collected in refugee camps in Darfur, a team from the World Health Organization [WHO] estimated that 10,000 of these refugees died each month between the end of 2003 and October 2004—mostly of malnutrition and disease linked to the violence. By March 2005, when the survey was released, the total number had risen to 200,000 deaths, the WHO later estimated.

The figures have not been thoroughly updated since. Yet fighting has worsened in the past few months.

That has led some researchers and human rights advocates to contend that the estimate of 200,000 killed since 2003 is too low. They say the violence has continued at the same or greater level each month since March 2005, meaning total deaths now could be as high as 400,000.

Government attacks in the last month alone have chased at least 60,000 from their homes, Rajasingham said, and dozens of villages have been razed. But aid agencies do not have time and resources to "go around counting the graves," he said, because they need to focus on survivors.

"We are concerned with the numbers of the living more than the number of the dead," Rajasingham said. "Our priority is to prevent further killing."

U.N. officials still usually use the 200,000 number. The Associated Press also uses the figure of at least 200,000 dead, based on the WHO survey.

For its part, Sudan's government in Khartoum says death tolls have been vastly inflated.

Sudanese President Omar al-Bashir said in September that only 10,000 people had died because of violence in Darfur since 2003. In a press conference this week, he lowered his figure to 9,000. "I challenge anybody to prove differently," al-Bashir said.

Differing Estimates of Victims

Khartoum denies having orchestrated killings in Darfur, and recently described attacks by Arab nomads called janjaweed as being conducted by "renegade Arab bandits" it does not control.

But academics who study the Darfur crisis put little stock in Khartoum's estimate.

They say the exact extent of Darfur's killing cannot be proven because the survey done by the WHO ended in March 2005 and no other research has been permitted on the ground by the Sudanese government since then.

David Nabarro, who directed the WHO survey, said that because of lack of freedom of movement and security concerns at the time, "we may not have been able to get the full extent of the violent mortality"—or those killed in violence.

"So the numbers are possibly higher," he said in a recent phone interview.

Nabarro stressed that his survey also described only "what was happening in a defined time frame (from end of 2003 until early 2005) and within accessible areas" of Darfur.

More than a dozen other studies have estimated death tolls ranging around 400,000 for the period since 2003.

Those include a survey by the Washington-based and State Department-funded Center for International Justice, which conducted interviews with Darfur refugees in Chad in August 2004. That survey found 61% of those interviewed reported witnessing the killing of a family member.

The survey combined that percentage with the number of refugees in Chad to reach a total of 200,000 dead in violent attacks. Because the WHO study did not survey refugees in Chad and did not count many violent deaths, the report argues the 200,000 that it estimated dead by violence among refugee families in Chad should be added to the WHO's toll of 200,000 dead inside Darfur camps to reach a total of 400,000 deaths.

But not all researchers accept the methodology, calling the extrapolation method faulty.

A Tenuous Peace Agreement for Darfur Is Reached

International Crisis Group

In early 2006, the Sudanese government met with leaders of rebel groups based in the southern region of the country. The purpose of the meeting, held in Abuja, Nigeria, was to secure an agreement to bring peace to Darfur. The effort enjoyed the support of the African Union—which had a tentative ceasefire agreement reached in 2005—and represented the continuing pressure from the international community to end the humanitarian crisis in Darfur. Eventually, Sudan's leaders signed a Darfur Peace Agreement (DPA) with some of the rebel leaders. But, according to the scholars and experts of the International Crisis Group who authored the following selection, the 2006 DPA was limited and had two major shortcomings. First, not all rebel factions signed it. Although Minni Minawi's Sudan Liberation Army (SLA) was a party to the agreement, other factions of the SLA, as well as the Justice and Equality Movement

SOURCE. "Darfur's Fragile Peace Agreement," *International Crisis Group*, June 20, 2006. Reproduced by permission.

rejected it. Second, the DPA did not do enough to require the Sudanese government to reign in the Janjaweed militias who were at the heart of much of Darfur's instability. The report goes on to offer suggestions, such as the involvement of a substantial United Nations peacekeeping force. The International Crisis Group is a non-governmental organization formed to provide analysis on security and human rights issues to governments and international organizations.

The Darfur Peace Agreement (DPA) signed under African Union (AU) auspices on 5 May 2006 between Sudan's government and the faction of the insurgent Sudan Liberation Army led by Minni Arkou Minawi (SLA/MM) is a first step toward ending the violence but strong, coordinated action is needed if it is to take hold. The document has serious flaws, and two of the three rebel delegations did not accept it. Fighting between rebel and government forces is down somewhat but violence is worse in some areas due to clashes between SLA factions, banditry, and inter-tribal feuds, while the Chad border remains volatile. If the DPA is not to leave Darfur more fragmented and conflict-prone than before, the international community must rapidly take practical measures to shore up its security provisions, improve prospects for the displaced to return home, bring in the holdouts and rapidly deploy a robust UN [United Nations] peacekeeping force with Chapter VII authority [which gives the UN broad peacekeeping abilities].

Resistance to the Agreement

Two parties to the negotiations in Abuja [Nigeria]—the SLA faction of Abdel Wahid Mohamed Nur (SLA/AW) and the Justice and Equality Movement (JEM)—have refused to sign. Abdel Wahid demands more direct SLA participation in implementation of security arrangements and is also dissatisfied with the DPA's provisions

for political representation and a victim's compensation fund. JEM maintains that the protocols on power and wealth sharing do not adequately address the conflict's root causes: the structural inequities between Sudan's centre and its periphery that led to the rebellion in 2003. Indeed, the DPA has accelerated the break-up of the insurgency into smaller blocs along loose ethnic lines.

Broadening buy-in and implementation of the security protocols will either make or break the peace in the short term. Maximum use needs to be made of the opportunity provided by the Darfur-Darfur Dialogue and Consultation, a communal reconciliation process prescribed by the DPA, to get acceptance of the agreement from segments of the population that were not represented in Abuja. Women's full participation will be important.

Majzoub Al-Khalifa (center), head of the Sudanese government's delegation, speaks at the Sudan peace talks in Abuja, Nigeria. Not all factions signed the Darfur Peace Agreement, causing further splintering of rebel groups. (AP Photo/ Sunday Alamba.)

The African Union

Recent decades have seen the growth of a number of multinational organizations. They include the North American Free Trade Agreement (NAFTA), which ties together the economies of the United States, Mexico, and Canada, and the Association of Southeast Asian Nations, or ASEAN, which seeks both political and economic cooperation. The European Union (EU), meanwhile, is rising to be a global power in its own right. African nations have continued the trend of building multi-country groups sharing common regional interests with the formation of the African Union.

The African Union (AU) was formed in July 2002, the successor to an earlier organization known as the Organization of African Unity. It is based in Addis Ababa, the capital of the East African Nation of Ethiopia, but it also maintains administrative offices in Gambia and South Africa. Of the fifty-four nations on the African continent, fifty-three are members of the AU, with Morocco being the one exception. A few countries are currently suspended for violating AU understandings having to do with political transitions and stability. As is the case with many other multinational entities, large, powerful, or wealthy nations such as South Africa and Nigeria often exert a disproportionate influence in the AU. As of 2010,

Keeping the Promise to Disarm

Security will not improve, however, unless [Sudanese capital] Khartoum disarms its proxy Janjaweed [roving gunmen, translates to "devil on horseback"] forces, a commitment it has already broken on five occasions. Though there are formal guarantors to the agreement and provisions in the security arrangements designed to help reinforce it, the DPA offers no effective guarantees on implementation. The AU Mission in Sudan (AMIS) is already overstretched and lacks the capacity to perform the additional monitoring and verification duties now asked of it. The DPA also does not address the takeover of peacekeep-

> The [UN] Security Council should apply sanctions that target any side, including the government, that violates the ceasefire.

its leader as head of the AU Assembly is Bingu wa Mutharika, an official from Malawi.

The AU has taken on large responsibilities and maintains large ambitions which go so far as envisioning both a common government, a sort of United States of Africa, and a common currency to be known as the Afro. Among its key subdivisions are the Pan-African Parliament, designed to encourage democratic institutions, and the African Court of Justice. AU leaders are also taking steps to manage the diversity of the continent by trying to choose, for example, between continent-wide economic integration or focusing instead on particular economic regions such as the Arab states of North Africa or the Swahili-speaking states of East Africa.

In 2004, as a result of a United Nations resolution on Darfur, the AU sent a peacekeeping force into Darfur to try to dampen the crisis there. Many of the troops—which ultimately numbered around 7,000—came from the nations of Nigeria, Ghana, and Rwanda. The AU's peacekeeping force in Darfur was supplemented in 2007 by a larger UN peacekeeping force. The organization has also sent troops to Somalia and maintains the prerogative to intervene elsewhere when necessary.

ing operations by the UN, which is daily becoming more necessary. Khartoum continues to obstruct and delay the planning process for that UN mission. If AMIS and then UN peacekeepers must ask the government's permission at every step, they will not be able to create the confidence refugees and displaced persons (IDPs) need to go home.

Current scenarios envisage a further six to nine months before the UN force is deployed. Many policymakers recognise that is unacceptably slow, because it means more deaths and no refugee and IDP returns, but have been reluctant to suggest more effective alternatives. The following steps are urgently required:

- The [UN] Security Council should apply sanctions that target any side, including the government, that violates the ceasefire or attacks civilians, peacekeepers, or humanitarian operations.

- The AU should spare no effort to widen acceptance of the DPA by all stakeholders, including by maintaining the dialogue with the SLA/Abdel Wahid faction and seeking further compromises on power and wealth-sharing issues, and its international partners, including the U.S. and the European Union (EU), should provide the political and financial backing that is needed for a successful Darfur-Darfur Dialogue and Consultation.

- The UN and other international partners should assist the AU in immediately strengthening AMIS by providing resources, logistical support, and technical expertise, and troop contributing countries in Africa should bring the force up to its authorised ceiling, so it can better carry out its current mandate as well as the additional tasks in the DPA.

- The Security Council should authorise deployment of a robust UN force, starting with a rapid reaction component, to take over from AMIS by 1 October 2006, with a clear Chapter VII mandate to use all necessary means to protect civilians and assist in the implementation of the DPA, including to act militarily as necessary to contain or neutralise Janjaweed, rebel, and hardline government spoilers.

- The EU and NATO [North Atlantic Treaty Organization] should work with the UN and the AU to ensure that the peacekeeping force has the capability to react rapidly to ceasefire violations or provocations by any party, and countries with advanced military capabilities should detail senior officers to the headquarters of the peacekeeping force to bolster its professionalism.

Despite Claims to the Contrary, the Fighting in Darfur Continues

Andrew Heavens

In July 2007, the United Nations Security Council agreed to a resolution designed to help bring peace and order to Darfur. The agreement involved sending a UN peacekeeping force to the region to supplement the one the African Union already had in place. The resulting African Union-United Nations Hybrid Mission in Darfur (UNAMID) provided a large force of more than thirty thousand soldiers and police involved in various duties that, officials hoped, would provide a peaceful environment for further talks between the Sudanese government and various rebel groups.

According to journalist Andrew Heavens, the author of the following selection, both Sudanese and UNAMID leaders proclaimed the mission to be highly successful as of the summer of 2009, having reduced the warfare in the region to little more than "banditry." Heavens also writes, however, that Western dip-

SOURCE. Andrew Heavens, "Sudan's Darfur No Longer at War—Peacekeeping Chief," *Reuters*, August 27, 2009. Reproduced by permission.

lomats and other observers, including a Darfurian rebel leader connected to the Justice and Equality Movement (JEM), view the fighting as ongoing and any peace negotiations as stalled. Andrew Heavens grew up in Africa and is a journalist based in Khartoum, Sudan.

Sudan's Darfur region is no longer in a state of war and only has one rebel group capable of mounting limited military campaigns, the head of the area's peacekeeping force said as he ended his tour of duty.

The statement was quickly dismissed by Darfur insurgents on Thursday [August 27, 2009] who said they were armed and preparing to launch new attacks on Sudan government troops in the near future.

The commander of the joint U.N./African Union UNAMID [African Union-United Nations Hybrid Mission in Darfur] peacekeeping force, Martin Luther Agwai, told reporters the conflict had now descended into banditry and "very low intensity" engagements that could still blight the remote western region for years without a peace deal.

"As of today, I would not say there is a war going on in Darfur," he said in a briefing in [Sudan's capital] Khartoum late on Wednesday.

"Militarily there is not much. What you have is security issues more now. Banditry . . . people trying to resolve issues over water and land at a local level. But real war as such, I think we are over that."

The six-year Darfur conflict has pitted pro-government militias and troops against mostly non-Arab rebels, who took up arms in 2003, demanding better representation and accusing Khartoum of neglecting the development of the region.

Khartoum says 10,000 have died in Darfur, while the United Nations puts the death count at up to 300,000.

Agwai became the latest senior figure to appear to play down the level of violence in Darfur, where the

Photo on following page: Although the armed conflict had decreased by 2009, the Sudanese Justice and Equality Movement claimed it still had the power to fight and hold territory. (Stuart Price/AFP/Getty Images.)

conflict has mobilised activists who accuse Khartoum of genocide.

Mostly Western campaigners and some diplomats were angered by comments in April by UNAMID's political leader Rodolphe Adada, who said Darfur had subsided into a "low-intensity conflict"; and by U.S. Sudan envoy Scott Gration in June who said he had seen the "remnants of genocide" in the region, stopping short, they said, of describing a current genocide.

> 'You don't say there is no war because there is no fighting for a week.'

Factions

Agwai said the fierce fighting of the early years of the conflict had subsided as rebel groups split into rival groups.

"Apart from JEM, I do not see any other group that can launch an attack on the ground," he said referring to the Justice and Equality Movement, a rebel force that launched an unprecedented attack on Khartoum last year.

Agwai said JEM could still fight, but did not have the manpower to hold territory. The Nigerian general added there was still a chance full blown conflict would resume.

JEM has clashed a number of times with the Sudanese army in the past months, and has said it withdrew voluntarily on two occasions to protect locals from government air attacks.

JEM leader Khalil Ibrahim on Thursday told Reuters there had been a period of calm in Darfur. "But this is the quiet period before the storm. In the coming days he (Agwai) will find out he is wrong. He is just talking like a politician and trying to show he was a success in Darfur."

Darfur Is Still Dangerous

Ibrahim said there were fewer battles now than in the early days of the conflict. "The quality of war has changed. The fighting is more intense. You don't say there is no war because there is no fighting for a week."

Jerry Fowler, head of Save Darfur, a U.S.-based advocacy group, said, "Darfur remains a very dangerous place"—above all for the millions of displaced people in camps.

He said that as recently as February there was a major battle between JEM and Sudanese government forces around the town of Muhajiriya.

Agwai, who is due to leave Sudan on Thursday after two years at the head of the peacekeeping force, said his main regret was the lack of progress in getting a peace deal.

"I really didn't have any peace so I couldn't command a force that could really keep the peace," he said, adding that Darfur's localised insecurity could continue "for years" without a settlement. Negotiations between JEM and Khartoum in Doha [Qatar] are stalled and the founder of Darfur's rebel Sudan Liberation Movement is refusing to talk.

CHAPTER 2

Controversies over the Crisis in Darfur

The United Nations Determines that the Killings in Darfur Do Not Constitute Genocide

Colum Lynch

An unknown number of civilians have died because of the crisis in Darfur. Among the controversies that have arisen is whether the death toll, and the methods by which it was achieved, amount to a genocide requiring strong intervention on the part of the global community. The word "genocide" was coined in the aftermath of and in reference to the Holocaust perpetrated by Nazi Germany against Europe's Jewish population during World War II when some 6 million Jews were systematically killed. In 1948, three years after the war ended, the United Nations devised a legal definition of genocide. One important feature was that a government show a clear intent to destroy a large population. In the following selection, *Washington Post* writer

Photo on previous page: UN soldiers stand guard in El-Fasher, North Darfur. Some favored the intervention of international forces, including soldiers drawn from African countries. (**Ashraf Shazly/ AFP/Getty Images.**)

SOURCE. Colum Lynch, "U.N. Panel Finds No Genocide in Darfur but Urges Tribunals," *Washington Post*, February 1, 2005, p. A01. Copyright © 2005, The Washington Post. Reprinted with permission.

Colum Lynch reports that the UN decided in 2005 that the sufferings of Darfur did not rise to the level of genocide because they could not find such a clear intent in the Sudanese government's policies and actions toward Darfur. However, the UN found that Sudan had likely committed major "crimes against humanity" and that a proper international response might be investigations or tribunals by the International Criminal Court. In contrast, in 2004 then-U.S. Secretary of State Colin Powell took the position that the situation in Darfur was indeed genocide.

UNITED NATIONS, Jan. 31—A U.N. [United Nations] commission investigating atrocities in Sudan has concluded that the government did not pursue a policy of genocide in the Darfur region but that [Sudan's capital] Khartoum and government-sponsored Arab militias known as the Janjaweed engaged in "widespread and systematic" abuse that may constitute crimes against humanity.

> The Sudanese justice system . . . 'is unable or unwilling' to address the situation in Darfur.

The five-member U.N. commission of inquiry "strongly recommends" that the U.N. Security Council invite the International Criminal Court to pursue a war crimes prosecution against those suspected of the worst abuse. The Sudanese justice system, it concluded, "is unable or unwilling" to address the situation in Darfur.

Photo on following page: A small child requires medical attention after receiving a head wound in a gun battle. Although the UN commission recognized the high level of violence and mayhem, it did not find that genocide had occurred. (AP Photo/ Marcus Bleasdale/VII.)

Targeted Violence

The 177-page report documents a concerted campaign of violence directed primarily at Darfur's black African Fur, Masalit, Jebel, Aranga and Zaghawa tribes. Since the violence began in early February 2003, more than 70,000 people have died from violence and resulting disease, and more than 1.8 million have been driven from their homes.

The United Nations Genocide Convention

In December 1948, the General Assembly of the United Nations passed UN General Assembly Resolution 260, or the Convention on the Prevention and Punishment of the Crime of Genocide. The measure has since been adopted by the majority of the members of the UN. Known more familiarly as the UN Genocide Convention, Resolution 260 remains the major basis for the understanding and condemnation of genocide.

The word "genocide" was coined by the Polish Jewish lawyer Rafael Lemkin during World War II. It combines two root words, one from Latin and one from Greek, and roughly means "race killing." Lemkin was also instrumental in making the subject of genocide important to the United Nations, which was itself formed in only 1945. In that period the world had recently grown aware of Nazi Germany's World War II Holocaust against European Jews in which six million were subjected to "race killing." But both Lemkin and, in time, the UN, recognized other similar episodes in recent history.

Political and diplomatic compromises resulted in the UN Genocide Convention making a fairly clear and specific definition of the term. A geno-

The commission's work is the most extensive international effort yet to document the atrocities in Darfur and to analyze their legal implications. In doing so, the commission was more cautious on the question of whether the violence amounted to genocide, the position taken by former U.S. secretary of state Colin L. Powell.

Nevertheless, the commission set the stage Monday for international war crimes prosecutions, charging the government and the Janjaweed of engaging in violence that included murder, torture, kidnapping, rape, forced displacement and the destruction of villages.

Senior U.S. officials said the commission's findings were serious enough to prosecute rights abusers as war criminals, despite the panel's decision not to declare that genocide had occurred. A finding of genocide—an attempt to systematically destroy a nation or ethnic

cide involves the "intent to destroy, in whole or in part, a national, ethnical, racial or religious group." The definition excludes the massacres of political enemies, and it also must feature the clear "intent" on the part of governments or their agents, to engage in such killings or in creating the conditions in which large numbers of deaths occur. The Convention further establishes criteria for condemning, or even putting on trial, those officials accused of involvement in genocide.

Despite the vast number of deaths that resulted from the crisis in Darfur beginning in 2003, the stance of the United Nations is that the events do not rise to the level of genocide. Their reasoning is that Sudanese officials did not show sufficient "intent" to massacre victims. In fact, the UN Genocide Convention has only been considered to have been breached twice since 1948, with both offenses coming in the 1990s. One was the attempted ethnic cleansing of Bosnians by Serbia in the aftermath of the breakup of the former Yugoslavia and the other the massacres that resulted from the Rwandan Civil War.

group—would have been considered a more powerful and symbolic statement, experts said, but its practical and legal impact would not have been significantly different from the commission's finding of possible crimes against humanity.

"Our interest here is accountability for the perpetrators of the atrocities, and there are obviously various ways that can be achieved," said Anne W. Patterson, acting U.S. representative to the United Nations.

The report's author, Antonio Cassese of Italy, said the commission placed the names of suspected war criminals, and the supporting evidence of their crimes, in a sealed file that will be presented to a future prosecutor.

The report's long-anticipated release precedes what many expect will be an intensified political battle in the Security Council over how to pursue such prosecution.

U.N. Secretary General Kofi Annan and European governments on the council want the International Criminal Court [ICC], based in The Hague [Netherlands], to oversee prosecution of Sudan's alleged war criminals. "This is a case which is tailor-made for the ICC," said Emyr Jones Parry, Britain's U.N. ambassador.

Disagreement on Seeking Justice

But the United States opposes the ICC and wants to create a new African court to handle the prosecutions. The [George W.] Bush administration refuses to recognize the legitimacy of the ICC out of concern that U.S. citizens could be subject to politically motivated charges before it.

Pierre-Richard Prosper, the U.S. ambassador at large for war crimes, has cautioned European supporters of the ICC not to force the Bush administration into a "thumbs-up or thumbs-down" vote in the council on an ICC prosecution.

Instead, he sought to rally support for a new tribunal in Tanzania that would be headed by the African Union and supported by the United Nations.

Stuart Holliday, the U.S. representative to the United Nations for special political affairs, said: "We're still in the process of discussing a variety of options, including with our African colleagues."

The violence in Darfur began in February 2003, when rebels from the Sudanese Liberation Army and the Justice and Equality Movement took up arms against the government. Khartoum organized and equipped the Arab militias known as the Janjaweed, which participated in a counterinsurgency campaign aimed at expelling many of the region's black tribes.

Khidir Haroun Ahmed, Sudan's ambassador to the United States, did not respond to a request to comment Monday before the report's release. But the Sudanese government has long denied that it has targeted civilians as part of its military campaign against the rebels.

The U.N. commission's report said a court could still determine that government officials or militia leaders did commit acts "with genocidal intent." But the panel found that "the crucial element of genocidal intent appears to be missing" from policy pursued by the government. "Generally speaking," it said, "the policy of attacking, killing and forcibly displacing members of some tribes does not evince a specific intent to annihilate, in whole or in part, a group distinguished on racial, ethnic, national or religious grounds."

That, however, should not "detract from the gravity of the crimes perpetrated" in Darfur, the report said, adding that they may be "no less serious and heinous than genocide."

Calling the Crisis in Darfur a Genocide or Not Is a Matter of Language, Not Reality

Gerard Prunier

In the following selection, scholar Gerard Prunier examines the common explanations behind the crisis in Darfur and whether it amounts to a genocide. He rejects the notion that it is simply the result of ethnic conflicts, since the central Sudanese government is so deeply involved. Prunier accepts, however, that the crisis can be understood as a form of "genocide" while acknowledging that a strict definition of the term can be difficult to reach. Indeed, while the United States has consistently claimed that a genocide was underway in Darfur, the United Nations stopped short of such a claim. In any case, Prunier

SOURCE. Gerard Prunier, *Darfur: The Ambiguous Genocide*. Ithaca, NY: Cornell University Press, 2007. Copyright © 2005 and 2007 by Gerard Prunier. Used by permission of the publisher, Cornell University Press.

notes, such arguments are academic and semantic, and they have less meaning in the context of the widespread suffering so many Darfurians have endured. Gerard Prunier is a French scholar of East Africa and the author of a number of books on the region.

B asically there are four types of explanations given to the Darfur violence.

The first is that it was an explosion of tribal conflicts exacerbated by drought. This was usually (but not always) a GoS [Government of Sudan] explanation. Secondly, it is explained as a counter-insurgency campaign gone badly wrong because the GoS used inappropriate means to fight back the JEM [Justice and Equality Movement] and SLM [Sudan Liberation Movement] insurrection. This is roughly the position of the Darfur specialist Alex de Waal and a number of Western governments. De Waal does not use the argument to exonerate [Sudanese capital] Khartoum. However, the Western governments adopting this position usually minimize the responsibility of the GoS, preferring to talk of "errors". A third explanation is that it was a deliberate campaign of "ethnic cleansing", with the GoS trying to displace or eliminate "African" tribes in order to replace them by "Arab" ones which it feels would be more supportive of "Arab" rule in Khartoum. Finally, genocide began to be mentioned as an explanation in early 2004 by more militant members of the international community and was given a strong boost by [UN official] Mukesh Kapila's interview in March. This hypothesis was supported by evidence of systematic racial killings. It failed to explain why Khartoum would have picked such an obviously wrong moment. . . .

> 'Ethnic cleansing' and 'genocide' are closely related.

Defining "Genocide"

"Ethnic cleansing" and "genocide" are closely related. As a rough differentiation we could take "ethnic cleansing" to mean massive killings of a certain section of the population in order to frighten the survivors away and occupy their land but without the intent of killing them all. "Genocide" is more difficult to define. The December 1948 International Convention on the Prevention and Punishment of Crimes of Genocide says that what constitutes genocide is "deliberately inflicting on the group conditions of life calculated to bring about its physical destruction *in whole or in part*". I personally have used another definition of the word in my book on the Rwandese genocide [of the 1990s], namely a coordinated attempt to destroy a racially, religiously or politically pre-defined group in its entirety. I am attached to the notion of an attempt at total obliteration because it has a number of consequences which seem to be specific of a "true" genocide. First, the numbers tend to be enormous because the purge is thorough. Second, there is no escape. In the case of a racially defined group, the reason is obvious, but if the group is religiously defined, no conversions will be allowed. And if it is politically defined, no form of submission will save its members. Finally, the targeted group will retain for many years after the traumatic events a form of collective paranoia which will make even its children live with an easily aroused fear. This is evident among the Armenians, the Jews and the Tutsi. But it is present also in less obviously acute forms in groups such as the North American Indians, French Protestants and Northern Irish Catholics. It is this "fractured consciousness" which makes future reconciliation extremely difficult.

> The horror experienced by the targeted group remains the same, no matter which word we use.

If we use the December 1948 definition it is obvious that Darfur is a genocide, but if we use the definition I proposed in my book on Rwanda it is not. At the immediate existential level this makes no difference; the horror experienced by the targeted group remains the same, no matter which word we use. But this does not absolve us from trying to understand the nature of what is happening. Unfortunately, whether the "big-G word" is used or not seems to make such a difference. It is in fact a measure of the jaded cynism of our times that we seem to think that the killing of 250,000 people in a genocide is more serious a greater tragedy and more deserving of our attention than that of 250,000 people in non-genocidal massacres. The reason seems to be the overriding role of the media coupled with the mass-consumption need for brands and labels. Things are not seen in their reality but in their capacity to create brand images, to warrant a "big story", to mobilize TV time high in rhetoric. "Genocide" is big because it carries the Nazi label, which sells well. "Ethnic cleansing" in next-best (though far behind) because it goes with Bosnia, which was the last big-story European massacre. But simple killing is boring, especially in Africa.

For Darfur the only reasonable position when faced with such sensationalism and verbal inflation is that adopted by ICG [International Crisis Group] President Gareth Evans or USAID [United States Agency for International Development] Director Roger Winter, who drew attention to the horror without entering into the semantic quarrel over whether or not it was genocide. The term "ethnic cleansing" was first used in connection with Darfur in a BBC commentary on 13 November 2003 and it soon expanded into the accusation of genocide. The difference between the proponents of the "ethnic cleansing" view of Darfur and those who insisted that it was a "genocide" largely had to do with the size of the killings:

> The current phrase of choice among diplomats and UN officials is "ethnic cleansing": but given the nature and

The 1990s Genocide in Rwanda

The African nation of Rwanda lies south of Sudan, with the nation of Uganda separating the two. In the mid-1990s, Rwanda was the scene of perhaps the most horrific mass killings of recent years. While the United Nations has hesitated to refer to the killings and deaths in Darfur as a genocide perpetrated by the government of Sudan and its agents, it had no hesitation in judging the events in Rwanda a genocide. Around 800,000 Rwandans, some 20 percent of the nation's population, were killed, mostly in 1994.

The Rwandan genocide was an effect of the Rwandan Civil War, which began in 1990. That year the Rwandan government, controlled by officials from a tribal group known as Hutus, began to fight with rebel organizations belonging to a separate tribe known as Tutsis. The two tribes maintained a long history of animosity, with conflicts stretching back decades and even reaching across borders into such neighboring nations as Botswana.

Indecisive fighting resulted in attempts to reach a ceasefire between the Hutu government and Tutsi rebels in 1993 but, the next year, the nation's president, Juvenal Habyarimana, was assassinated. Hutu leaders blamed the rebels for the assassination and used it as a pretext to launch genocidal attacks on Tutsi populations by government-backed militia groups. (A French investigation later suggested that the leader of the Tutsi rebels, Paul Kagame, was in fact largely responsible for Habyarimana's assassination.) From April to July 1994, these militias massacred hundreds of thousands of Tutsi. The massacres had apparently been planned for some time, should an opportunity arise, with the Hutu employing extensive racial and ethnic stereotypes to further the hatred between the two groups. Most of the killings took place in the victims' own villages by rifle or machete, with the bodies disposed of hastily in mass graves or, sometimes, simply left behind.

The response of the United Nations, the United States, and the global community as a whole was slow, although the French, who had longstanding ties with the region, tried to intervene and set up refugee camps for Tutsi escapees. The takeover of Rwanda in 1995 by the Tutsi rebels, meanwhile, inspired Hutus to also escape, and refugees from both groups continue to be the source of instability in neighboring nations such as Burundi and Congo (previously known as Zaire). Tens of thousands of Rwandans, from both groups, have died in refugee camps from disease and hunger.

In November 1994, the UN Security Council passed a resolution condemning the genocide in Rwanda and establishing an International Criminal Court to try those responsible. The trials have continued into 2010.

scale of human destruction and the clear racism animating attacks systematically directed against civilians from the African tribal groups, the appropriate term is "genocide".

The notion of "ethnic cleansing", implying that the GoS had been trying to displace African tribes in order to give their land to "Arabs", is not backed by any evidence other than the shouts hurled at the victims by the perpetrators themselves. Although they (the perpetrators) might have hoped for such an outcome of the massacres, it is doubtful that a policy of that kind had been clearly thought out in Khartoum. This does not exclude the possibility that some in the GoS might have wished for that outcome, but the few instances of "Arabs" settling on the land abandoned by African peasants do not seem very convincing. The "Arabs" are mostly nomads who do not seem much interested in becoming agriculturalists.

Early American Opinions

As for the most prominent user of the word "genocide" in connection with Darfur, the former US Secretary of State Colin Powell seems to have based himself on the December 1948 definition of the word when he said on 9 Septemher 2004 that in his opinion Darfur was a genocide. Other spokesmen for world opinion danced a strange ballet around the "big-G word": President George W. Bush declared: "Our conclusion is that a genocide is underway in Darfur." His electoral opponent John Kerry concurred: it was "the second genocide in ten years". The British Minister of State for Foreign Affairs Chris Mullin was more prudent, merely saying that a genocide "might have taken place". The spokesman for the French Foreign Ministry limited himself to saying that there had been "massive violations of human rights", while Walter Lindner, for the German Foreign Affairs Ministry, said that this was "a humanitarian tragedy . . . with a potential

U.S. secretary of state Colin Powell (left) joined the Sudan minister of foreign affairs Mustafa Osman Esmail in Khartoum, Sudan. Powell said in 2004 that the conflict in Darfur did rise to the level of genocide. (Marco Longari/ AFP/Getty Images.)

for genocide". In the end none of them went beyond talk. The UN, the AU [African Union] and the humanitarians were left holding the bloody babies.

The United Nations' Choice

This leaves open the question of "intent" which was at the centre of the UN Commission of Inquiry's decision not to call Darfur a genocide. The report apparently wrote that there was "not sufficient evidence to indicate that Khartoum had a state policy intended to exterminate a particular racial or ethnic group", a definition that moved away from that of December 1948, but which in itself is acceptable. However, the semantic play ended up being an evasion of reality. The notion that this was probably not a "genocide" in the most strict sense of the word seemed to satisfy the Commission that things were not really too bad. But conclusions about "war crimes" could, if actually carried over into IPC [International Police Commission] indictments, for once have serious consequences.

The U.S. Should Be Ready to Take Strong Measures Against the Sudanese Government

John Prendergast

The following selection is taken from testimony on the Darfur crisis given before the Foreign Affairs Committee of the U.S. House of Representatives by writer and human rights leader John Prendergast. The day before the hearing, President George W. Bush had used the setting of Washington D.C.'s United States Holocaust Memorial Museum to reiterate the U.S.'s policy of negotiating with Sudan's government. Prendergast was disappointed and suggested that the United States must instead take a more "muscular" approach toward Sudan in order to solve the crisis in Darfur. He notes that Sudan's leaders are unlikely to take mere "negotiation" seriously but would likely respond to stronger measures, including elements of military action. John Prendergast is the author of eight books on Africa and was

SOURCE. John Prendergast, "Darfur Hearing," House Committee on Foreign Affairs, April 19, 2007. Reproduced by permission of John Prendergast.

director of African Affairs in President Bill Clinton's National Security Council. He is also the founder of the Enough Project, an activist organization focusing on humanitarian issues.

Thank you, Mr. Chairman and members of this esteemed Committee, for the opportunity to share my views on the world's hottest war and what our role should be in ending it.

Yesterday morning [April 18, 2007], the auditorium at the Holocaust Museum was tense with anticipation. President [George W.] Bush was there to make what was to be a major announcement on U.S. policy towards Darfur. Holocaust survivor Elie Wiesel was invited to be with him, underscoring the gravity of the event. And the administration had been leaking for months about its threatened "Plan B" policy.

> Barking without biting is the diplomatic equivalent of giving comfort to the enemy.

Had the refugees and displaced Darfurians in [actor and activist] Mia Farrow's photographs been sitting in the audience yesterday, their disappointment would have been crushing. Instead of finally announcing what every activist and member of Congress has been demanding for the last three years—measures that would punish the regime for its orchestration of what the Bush administration repeatedly calls genocide—President Bush instead issued another set of dramatic warnings, another threat without a specific deadline for action.

Barking without biting is the diplomatic equivalent of giving comfort to the enemy. In this case, though, it may be even worse. Each time the administration has issued an empty threat over the past three years and then not enforced it, the Khartoum regime has been emboldened to escalate its destruction and obstruction in Darfur. If there is a Guinness Book of World Records entry for

> During the 18 years of its military rule, the regime in Khartoum has only responded to focused international and regional pressure.

most threats issued with no follow up, Darfur is likely setting a new standard.

After living in, studying or working in Sudan for the last 22 years, and having negotiated directly with Sudan's leadership during the Clinton administration, I can tell you that the regime no longer takes our speeches and our threats seriously, and will continue to flout international will until there are specific and escalating costs to their actions.

I do not tell that to you on a whimsical hope that it might be true. In these matters, I would much prefer to rely on empirical evidence. The preponderance of evidence shows that during the 18 years of its military rule, the regime in Khartoum has only responded to focused international and regional pressure. Three times the regime has reversed its position on a major policy issue, and each of those three times the change resulted from intensive diplomacy backed by serious pressure—two ingredients sadly and shockingly missing from the response to Darfur today, despite the stirring speeches. The three cases are the regime's support for international terrorist organizations during the early to mid 1990s; its support for slave-raiding militias in southwestern Sudan throughout the 1990s; and its prosecution of a war in southern Sudan that took two million Sudanese lives. . . .

Wanted: A Firm Deadline and a Real Plan B

Nearly everyone agrees on the necessary ingredients for the stabilization of Darfur:

- a peace agreement that addresses the remaining issues of the non-signatory rebels and broader Darfurian society; and

- an effective civilian protection force, the starting point for which is the "hybrid" AU-UN [African Union-United Nations] force which the entire world supports, except the Khartoum regime.

The disagreement begins around how to secure those two critical peace and protection objectives. These are the first two "P's" of what the ENOUGH Campaign calls the "3 P's" of crisis response. The third P is punishment: imposing a cost for the commission of mass atrocities and building leverage through these measures for securing the peace and protection objectives.

First, a credible timeline is crucial. One empty threat after another must be replaced with a firm deadline which will trigger automatic action. I join with the Save Darfur Coalition in calling for May 1 [2007] to be that deadline. The U.S. told UN Secretary General Ban

John Prendergast (center), activist and founder of ENOUGH, was arrested while protesting against the violence in Darfur outside the Sudanese embassy in Washington, D.C. (Chip Somodevilla/Getty Images.)

Ki-Moon that U.S. and UN Security Council [UNSC] sanctions would be delayed two to four weeks from the Secretary General's April 2 request to give diplomacy more time.

Though further delay is abhorrent, there is a silver lining. The Bush administration's current Plan B, the measures that President Bush was going to announce yesterday at the Holocaust Museum, is inadequate and must be buttressed in very specific ways. May 1 thus gives the administration enough time to prepare a real Plan B—a set of punitive measures with teeth.

Most of the measures the administration was prepared to announce were full of implementation holes and too minimalist to make a major impact on the calculations of regime officials in Khartoum, or on intransigent rebel leaders. After ten years of U.S. unilateral sanctions, the Sudanese government and its commercial partners have easily figured out how to circumvent any unilateral U.S. measures. With little support and cooperation from the CIA [Central Intelligence Agency] because of our close counter-terrorism cooperation with the very same Sudanese officials who are architects of the Darfur policy, U.S. policy-makers are largely in the dark about how the Sudanese government transacts its oil sector business, and can not identify most of the major Sudanese companies owned by regime officials and doing business throughout Europe, Asia and the Middle East. We simply don't know the names of the dozens of subsidiaries of existing Sudanese companies that can conduct transactions using U.S. dollars with total impunity.

What is needed is an intelligence surge from the CIA and an enforcement surge from the Treasury Department. Without new staff, none of the measures will be able to be enforced with the existing burdens related to other sanctioned regimes. Intelligence and enforcement surges will at least bring the U.S. up to speed on who is doing what and how to effectively implement any punitive measures. And without a clear strategy of rapidly escalating pressure through a variety of economic and legal measures, then the deadly status quo will no doubt prevail.

The point is not simply to punish for punishment's sake, although if the Bush administration's characterization of the atrocities in Darfur as genocide were meaningful, it would fulfill the Genocide Convention's requirement to punish the crime. Punitive measures are essential to building the leverage necessary to gain Khartoum's compliance for a durable peace deal for Darfur and the deployment of an effective international force to protect civilians. Similar measures should be imposed against leading rebel commanders and political leaders if they are deemed to have committed atrocities or are obstructing real and balanced peace efforts, which so far do not exist.

> Without a clear strategy of rapidly escalating pressure through a variety of economic and legal measures . . . the deadly status quo will no doubt prevail.

Any of the measures that the Bush administration is considering will be exponentially more effective if they are done multilaterally. The U.S. government already has strong unilateral sanctions in place against Sudan, barring U.S. companies from doing business with the National Congress Party (though allowing U.S. businesses to work with the Government of South Sudan), freezing assets in the U.S. of the Sudanese government and some Sudanese companies and individuals, and blocking financial transactions of companies registered in Sudan. These measures, enacted by the Clinton Administration in 1997, did affect the calculations of the regime in pursuit of policy objectives at the time, but have since run their course as the Sudanese regime circumvents U.S. institutions in its commercial dealings. Therefore, if these measures were applied multilaterally and expanded they would have a much bigger impact on the pocketbooks of those responsible for crimes against humanity. Moreover, the Government of Sudan will have a much more difficult time scoring propaganda points when the U.S. is not acting alone.

The following additional punitive measures could be implemented immediately without major cost, but it would require a strong diplomatic effort to rally multilateral support and significant increases in staffing and resources to ensure aggressive implementation.

- **Target Sudanese Officials Multilaterally:** Impose UN Security Council targeted sanctions—including asset freezes and travel bans—against persons responsible for crimes against humanity in Darfur. The existing U.S. effort would target three individuals. The number must be much higher. Such sanctions have been authorized in previous UNSC resolutions, and called for in multiple reports from the UNSC Sanctions Committee Panel of Experts.

- **Target Sudanese Companies Multilaterally**: Impose UN Security Council sanctions against the list of Sudanese companies already targeted unilaterally by the U.S., and establish a UN Panel of Experts to further investigate which companies are conducting the business necessary to underwrite Sudan's war machine.

- **Press International Banks to Stop Doing Business with Sudan**: As is the case with Iran, U.S. officials should engage with a number of international banking institutions to strongly encourage them to stop doing business with Sudan, with the implication being that if such business continues then all transactions by those banks with U.S. commercial entities (and those of other countries willing to work with us) would eventually be banned.

- **Support the ICC [International Criminal Court] Indictment Process:** Provide information and declassified intelligence to the International Criminal

Court to help accelerate the process of building indictments against senior officials in the regime for their role in orchestrating mass atrocities in Darfur. The U.S. has the most such intelligence and should come to agreement with the ICC about what information to share.

Punitive measures will demonstrate to those committing atrocities and those undermining peace efforts—whether a part of the government or a rebel group—that there will be a cost for their actions, and that cost will increase with each major human rights or diplomatic violation.

Wanted: A Serious Diplomatic Strategy

It is not enough for the U.S. to have a part-time Special Envoy and occasional visits by high level officials. The U.S. needs to have a team of diplomats working full time and globally to secure the following prerequisites for Sudan's stabilization:

- Support for the development of a common rebel negotiating position;
- Support for the negotiation of amendments to the Darfur Peace Agreement that address the reservations of the non-signatory rebels and broader Darfurian civil society;
- Support for addressing the spillover impacts of the conflict in Chad and the Central African Republic;
- Support for the implementation of the peace deal that ended the north-south war, a deal that is increasingly put at risk by Darfur's deterioration;
- Support for negotiations to end the war between the Ugandan government and the Lord's Resistance Army (LRA), which threatens to undermine peace in Sudan;

- Support for the international diplomacy (particularly with China, the EU [European Union], and the Arab League) necessary to see an effective civilian protection force deployed to Darfur, the starting point for which is the "hybrid" AU-UN proposal that Khartoum has not accepted.

In order to be successful, the White House needs to put forward a clear strategy and exert itself in the interagency process to improve cooperation and coordination between the government agencies with roles to play in implementing it. Intelligence officials must be put at the disposal of the peace efforts; Treasury Department officials must be planning and staffing for expanding punitive measures; Defense Department officials must be engaged in accelerated contingency military planning with their colleagues in NATO [the North Atlantic Treaty Organization], the EU and the UN; and the White House should be aggressively tasking various agencies and ensuring that the effort is taken as seriously as that of North Korea, Iran, and other important foreign policy priorities. . . .

> Newsflash: the emperor has no clothes.

Wanted: Military Planning and Action for Protection

Newsflash: the emperor has no clothes. Until there is recognition of the nakedness of the current international strategy to protect civilians, Darfurians will have no hope of getting that protection. To that end, pressure must be escalated on Khartoum to accept phase three of the UN/AU hybrid plan, the UN has to be pressed to prepare for the immediate implementation of phases one and two, and the Bush administration's budget (and the budgets of other major contributors to UN peacekeeping) must include adequate funding to resource the mission at full capacity. The President's current budget request is insufficient and suggests skepticism on the part of the administration that the mission will ever deploy. Finally, every effort should be made to amend the mandate of the existing and future mission to be one that prioritizes the protection of civilians.

President Paul Kagame of Rwanda, one of the largest troop contributors to the current AU force, told me recently that the hybrid force could be effective if sufficient resources were provided with a clear mandate. Regarding civilian protection, he said, "We would take on additional tasks if we had the resources and the mandate." In frustrating meetings about the impotent response of the broader international community, the Rwandan government has not ruled out withdrawing its troops from an increasingly toothless mission. "If we had more troops, the proper equipment, the right mandate, and a no-fly zone to paralyze the air force," President Kagame told me, "We could protect the civilian population of Darfur." With the proper logistics and resources, Kagame would be willing to consider doubling the number of Rwandan troops in Darfur, and concentrate them in areas immediately under threat. He said it was crucial that any military pressure be backed by a strong international policy of pressure and sanctions. "We don't want to be left hanging," he warned.

This is why UN Security Council financing of an enhanced Darfur deployment is key. With a stronger mandate and more funding for the critical logistical and equipment gaps that exist currently, more African troops would be offered to the AU mission, and the force on the ground would be much more effective.

The UN Security Council also should accelerate the deployment of protection elements to the border regions of Chad and Central African Republic [CAR], with mandates to protect at-risk communities, IDP settlements, and refugee camps. However, there is no military solution to Darfur and its spillover: a peace deal in Darfur is a prerequisite for a peacekeeping force to be effective and genuine political dialogue in Chad and CAR should accompany any deployment of international troops or police to those countries. Further, we must acknowledge that international troops or police in Chad and CAR will have little impact on the situation in Darfur. Only a political resolution in Darfur will help defuse the political tensions in Chad and CAR, not the other way around.

In terms of coercive military measures, there are two for which accelerated planning processes should commence within the NATO framework, with the understanding that any action would at least seek UN Security Council approval and only act in its absence if the situation deteriorated dramatically and all other avenues had been explored.

- **No Fly Zone:** absent an enhanced ground component, this option is questionable and fraught with potential negative side effects. However, it is important to press ahead with planning an enforcement mechanism for a No Fly Zone as the Sudanese regime continues to use aerial bombing as a central component of its military strategy and its civilian displacement objectives. If the mandate would be strengthened and more troops deployed to protect civilians, neutralizing the Sudanese regime's one tactical advantage will be essential.

- **Non-Consensual Force Deployment:** although few nations are likely to volunteer in the present context, if the situation dramatically deteriorates in Darfur (large-scale pullout of aid agencies, increasing attacks on camps or AU forces, etc.), the debate could shift quickly and credible plans need to be in place to move troops into the theater of war quickly with a primary focus on protecting vulnerable civilian populations.

Credible military planning should commence immediately for both options to demonstrate to Khartoum that decisive military action is possible in a short timeframe. Further planning should also be undertaken for the kinds of targeted military actions argued for by Congressman Donald Payne, Anthony Lake [former U.S. national security advisor], and Susan Rice [former assistant secretary of state of African affairs], and reinforced by Dr. Rice in her testimony last week in the Senate Foreign Relations Committee. This planning is both a practical necessity, and a means to build and utilize leverage against the regime.

The U.S. must move away from its current policy of constructive engagement without leverage (with gentle persuasion being the preferred tool) to a more muscular policy focused on walking softly and carrying—and using—a bigger stink. Unfulfilled threats and appeals should be replaced quickly with punitive measures backing a robust peace and protection initiative. We may not know the names of the victims in Darfur, but we know the names of the orchestrators of the policy that led to their deaths.

There is hope. The growing constituency in the U.S. focused on countering the atrocities in Darfur is expanding by the day, led by student, Jewish, Christian, and African-American organizations. Elected officials who ignore this crescendo of activism—though not usually front page news—do so at their own peril. This Congress will do a great service to all of history's genocide victims—on this day following the Holocaust Remembrance Day—if you make it politically costly for this administration, or any future one, to stand idly by while atrocities such as those in Darfur are being committed.

Only Sudan Can Take the Lead in Addressing the Darfur Crisis

Tanalee Smith

In the following selection from 2005, the Associated Press reports that Sudan had ended its two-decade southern civil war with the signing of a peace deal. The Sudanese government, caught in the excitement of the southern peace deal, vowed to focus on the crisis in Darfur. Amidst intense pressure from the international community, Sudan has promised to resolve the problems in Darfur as no international body can.

Sudan officially ends its two-decade southern civil war on Sunday [January 9, 2005] with the signing of a peace deal. Amid the jubilation lies the hope that ending one war may spark a solution to the country's

---

SOURCE. Tanalee Smith, "Sudan Hopes Peace Deal Ends Darfur Crisis," AP Online, January 8, 2005. Reproduced by permission.

second—in western Darfur, where an equally brutal conflict has led to a massive humanitarian crisis.

Sudan's president, caught up in the excitement of the long-awaited southern peace deal, has said he now would be willing to consider wealth- and power-sharing agreements with rebels in Darfur.

"The deal in the south puts Sudan on the doorstep of a new era of peace for the whole country," said Jean Baptiste Natama, a senior political officer with the African Union, which is mediating Darfur peace talks. "It is a means to the solution in Darfur, a necessary bridge."

But continued outbreaks of fighting in Darfur—despite repeated assurances from both sides to honor a recent cease-fire pledge—indicate just how difficult the problem might be to solve, even with new momentum.

The comprehensive peace deal for the southern war will be signed in Nairobi, Kenya. It comes after government and southern rebel officials on Dec. 31 concluded two years of peace talks by signing a permanent truce, and endorsed a detailed plan to end the conflict. It includes power- and wealth-sharing agreements and a proposed government for an autonomous southern Sudan.

[U.S.] Secretary of State Colin Powell traveled to Kenya on Saturday after touring the tsunami devastation in Asia. He was to attend Sunday's peace signing.

Peace in the Civil War Key to Darfur Solution

Even before the southern deal was reached, officials inside and outside Sudan had linked the two conflicts, saying peace in the civil war would be key to making progress on the so-far intractable Darfur front.

Efforts for a Darfur solution have gone in fits and starts—a Nov. 9 cease-fire signed in Abuja, Nigeria, between the government and the two main rebel groups has been repeatedly broken by both sides. And new in-

> In its new focus on peace, the Sudanese government has given assurances that it is serious about solving the Darfur crisis.

surgent groups have recently arisen to add strength to the resistance.

On Tuesday, the rebel Sudan Liberation Army accused government soldiers of attacking a base in North Darfur and threatened that rebels would step up military operations in retaliation.

Nevertheless, in its new focus on peace, the Sudanese government has given assurances that it is serious about solving the Darfur crisis.

Darfur is "definitely" next on the government's list of priorities, said Deputy Information Minister Abdel Dafe Khattib, saying the conclusion of the southern peace deal has brought a positive feeling.

"There is a different mood, one of trying to mend fences. I think it's going to help" with Darfur, he said. "The government itself is trying to mend fences with all factions, inside and out, be it American, European or our neighbors."

The southern deal was a result both of Western pressure and Sudan's desire to end its pariah status in the international community, said Charles Gurdon, an analyst with a British consultancy firm.

"If Libya and Iraq and others can come off the U.S. list of state sponsors of terrorism, Sudan also has to try," he said. "It is a calculated position—this way they can have more time to sort out western Sudan."

Photo on following page: South African president Thabo Mbeki favored maintaining Djibril Bassole (pictured), the Joint Chief Mediator, as the central negotiator in the Darfur conflict. (Ashraf Shazly/AFP/Getty Images.)

Importance of Darfur

He said Darfur was more important to the government than the south, because its population is Muslim, like most of the north, and because the bulk of the army comes from there.

However, the area never had much political nor economic power. It was that feeling of marginalization that led non-Arab rebel groups to take up arms in February

2003 against what they saw as years of state neglect and discrimination against Sudanese of African origin.

The government responded with a counterinsurgency campaign in which the Janjaweed, an Arab militia, has allegedly committed wide-scale abuses against the African population.

About 70,000 people have been killed from disease, hunger and attacks just since last March, and nearly 2 million are believed to have fled their homes. Many more are believed to have died in the fighting.

There are parallels with the southern crisis, in which rebels made up mainly of Christians and animists demanded greater autonomy from Sudan's Islamic-dominated government and a greater share of the country's wealth for the south. That war left more than 2.5 million people dead, mostly from hunger and disease, and has driven more than 4 million people from their homes.

The international community has put intense international pressure on Sudan to end the Darfur conflict, which the U.N. last year called the world's worst humanitarian crisis. Two U.N. Security Council resolutions have threatened possible sanctions, as has a bill signed by [U.S.] President [George W.] Bush in December.

Sudan's President Should Be Ostracized

Daniel K. Pryce

In the following selection, Daniel K. Pryce, a citizen of the West African nation of Ghana, argues that Ghana's president, John Kufuor, should not accept a diplomatic visit from Sudan's president, Omar al-Bashir. Such a visit, Pryce says, would be an insult to the many victims of the violence in Darfur and would amount to Ghana honoring a leader who could be considered a war criminal. Indeed, Pryce acknowledges the possibility that, should al-Bashir land on Ghanaian soil, he might be turned over to the International Criminal Court to face charges of war crimes. Pryce suggests that Ghanaians might feel a connection to the African victims of Sudan's largely Arab militias and that, as Ghana continues to build its own democratic structures, any official visit by al-Bashir would be a step backwards. A Ghanaian educated and living in the United States, Pryce is a columnist for modernghana.com.

SOURCE. Daniel K. Pryce, "Kufuor Must not Allow Omar al-Bashir on Ghanaian Soil!" modernghana.com, September 29, 2008. Reproduced by permission.

A September 23, 2008, news item published on Francis Akoto's GhanaHomePage, titled "Sudan's President to visit Ghana," the former the most influential and oft-accessed pro-Ghanaian Internet portal, at once rankled me and reignited my astoundingly waning passion to write again for my fellow Ghanaians. For those who know very little about Omar Hassan al-Bashir, Sudan's despotic leader, this man has superintended—overtly and covertly—some of the worst cases of carnage, dismemberment, gross sexual abuse and annihilation of large numbers of his country's black population, especially in the Darfur province, by the ostensibly "superior" Arab members of Sudanese society, which is the very reason why al-Bashir's planned visit to Ghana has both generated outrage among the peaceable people of our dear nation and received unequivocal denunciation.

> Al-Bashir's planned visit to Ghana has . . . generated outrage among the peaceable people of our dear nation.

For world leaders to altogether embrace the trajectory of ambivalence while our Sudanese brothers and sisters are massacred on a daily basis—the only "sins" of these "ostracized" members of Sudanese society are their Negroid features and a lack of access to political power—remains an even greater mystery than the carnage itself. Of course, some will argue that the vastly undermanned joint UN-AU [United Nations-African Union] Peacekeeping Force in place in Darfur has performed amply well in the last few years to repulse advancing Sudanese Army personnel and members of the notorious Janjaweed militia [roving gunmen, translates to "devil on horseback"]—the latter two have been receiving direct orders from Omar al-Bashir himself to perpetrate dastardly acts against the unarmed black Sudanese population—but could not the world have done more?

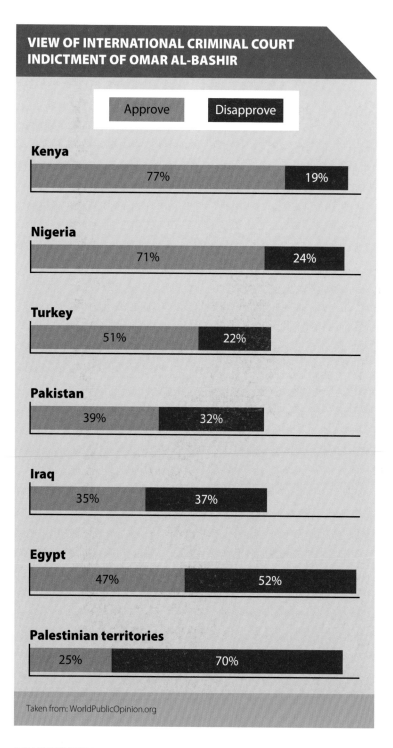

VIEW OF INTERNATIONAL CRIMINAL COURT INDICTMENT OF OMAR AL-BASHIR

Approve   Disapprove

Kenya
77%   19%

Nigeria
71%   24%

Turkey
51%   22%

Pakistan
39%   32%

Iraq
35%   37%

Egypt
47%   52%

Palestinian territories
25%   70%

Taken from: WorldPublicOpinion.org

Indifference or Exploitation from the World's Powers

Five years after the genocide in Darfur had begun, the world's leading nations, such as the U.S. and Great Britain, have done very little to protect the lives, livelihoods and dignity of these helpless Sudanese people, whose own government is determined to wipe them off the face of the earth! More importantly, China, a superpower in its own right, because of its unfettered access to Sudanese oil and markets, has refused to issue a statement

Omar al-Bashir

The current president of Sudan and a central—as well as controversial—figure in the crisis in Darfur is Omar al-Bashir. Having originally been raised to the president's office in 1989 as a result of a military coup d'état, al-Bashir was formally elected to the post in April 2010 when Sudan held its first national vote in many years.

Omar al-Bashir was born in 1944 into that part of Sudan's population that is of Arab heritage. He received much of his military training in Sudan's powerful neighbor to the north, Egypt, and returned to lead the coup that ousted Sadiq al-Mahdi in 1989. The regimes he has led have undergone important changes in name and nature although, on the whole, they have granted relatively strong influence to both Sudanese Arabs and to a conservative understanding of the Islamic religion. He has been consequently accused of marginalizing the non-Arab populations of Sudan's southern regions such as Darfur. He was also accused, in the 1990s, of supporting Islamist terrorist groups, although such accusations have since been tempered due to a lack of direct evidence.

Al-Bashir has presided over a long-lasting civil war in Sudan, which at its heart is a conflict between the Arab tribes of the north, who dominate the capital city of Khartoum, and the non-Arab tribes of the south and west. The non-Arabs generally share his Islamic faith (with important exceptions) but resent al-Bashir's alleged attempts to impose both Arabism and his strict reading of Islam. The civil war ended with a peace agreement reached in 2005. The agreement provided Southern Sudan with the ability to govern itself for six years, after which its residents would be permitted

of condemnation against the Khartoum administration, let alone intervene with resources and logistical support for the defense of the vulnerable black population. This writer still refuses to accept the reasons proffered by the world community for China's hosting of the recently concluded Olympic Games, for in my mind, China remains one of the greatest obstacles to peace in the Darfur region, more so because of both its alignment with the Khartoum administration and its veto power on the UN Security Council.

to vote on a more permanent form of independence. Although it is related to Sudan's civil war, the crisis in Darfur is more often understood as a distinct problem, the attempt by the Khartoum government to eliminate the ethnic problem presented by Darfurian tribes.

The violence and instability of his years in power, as well as his alleged connections to global terrorism, have made al-Bashir the focus of global controversy. The United States, for instance, bars American companies from doing business in Sudan, a position adopted in 1997. American military aircraft, in 1998, went so far as to bomb a Sudanese pharmaceutical plant as a purported blow against al-Bashir's ties to terrorism. In 2008 the International Criminal Court (ICC) issued an arrest warrant for al-Bashir, citing his personal responsibility in genocide, crimes against humanity, and war crimes in Darfur. Al-Bashir rejects the charges, maintaining that the human toll of the crisis in Darfur has been much exaggerated and that the ICC, as well as Western powers such as the United States, have targeted him unfairly. Although the ICC's warrant provides for the arrest of al-Bashir if he travels outside the country, to date no nation he has visited has chosen to take that step, and he pledges to always travel with the military protection of Sudanese Air Force jets.

In economic matters, al-Bashir's policies have helped to create a boom based mostly on foreign investment in natural resources such as oil. The great beneficiaries of this boom have been, apparently, Sudanese Arabs as well as those nations—most notably China—that have chosen not to mount sanctions on or ban doing business with al-Bashir's regime.

Currently, as a signatory to the International Criminal Court (ICC), headed by the Argentinean Luis Moreno-Ocampo, Ghana is bound by principle to respect the call of the afore-named august body to arrest any wanted criminal who lands on Ghanaian soil. As such, unless an arrest warrant has not been issued by the time Omar al-Bashir arrives in Ghana, should the Sudanese leader defy all logic and embark on this trip, Mr. al-Bashir faces a very real prospect of being arrested and handed over to the ICC, to be tried for crimes against humanity.

A War Criminal

The well-respected American news outlet, PBS, reports that Omar Al-Bashir has, over the last 5 years, supervised the annihilation of "at least 300,000 [black Sudanese] and forced another 2.5 million to flee their homes." PBS further reports that the Chief Prosecutor of the ICC, Luis Moreno-Ocampo, has "filed 10 charges against al-Bashir: three counts of genocide, five of crimes against humanity and two of murder." The world is thus anxiously waiting for the ICC to issue an order for the arrest of Omar al-Bashir, one of Africa's last pitbulls, a man with absolutely no regard for the lives of his fellow citizens, a man who has continually disregarded the call of the international community to rein in the thugs operating in the Darfur region.

A synopsis of events in Darfur—these acts of violence began in 2003—reveals that these attacks are almost always the work of "a coalition of militia and Sudanese military forces" (PBS.org). "Moreno-Ocampo [further states], 'These forces would then surround village[s] and on occasion, the Air Force would be called upon to drop bombs on the village[s] as a precursor to the attacks. The ground forces would then enter the village[s] or town[s] and attack civilian inhabitants. They kill men, children, elderly, women; they subject women and girls to massive rapes. They burn and loot the villages'" (as reported by

PBS.org). For those who would argue that it is a Sudanese problem only, they ought to remember that it is exactly such inactions and trivializations on the part of the larger world community, in the face of a compendium of horrific atrocities, which emboldened the likes of Germany's Adolf Hitler, Liberia's Charles Taylor and Serbia's Slobodan Milosevic to decimate large segments of their respective countries' populations.

Stories of Horror

Below are the accounts of just two of the tens of thousands of Sudanese rape victims. A 35-year-old mother of five, from South Darfur, reports that the "Janjaweed would pass their hands touching the heads and legs of women; if a woman has long hair and fat legs and silky skin she is immediately taken away to be raped. Some of us were raped in front of the crowd. Two of them [Janjaweed hooligans] came to me, I resisted them. . . .

Omar al-Bashir (in white) is president of Sudan, and many feel he should be charged with crimes against humanity. (Ashraf Shazly/AFP/Getty Images.)

They hit me and decided to rape me in front of others" (as reported by Human Rights Watch). According to another woman from North Darfur, the Janjaweed would "rape girls as young as seven or eight, while some women were raped and then genitally mutilated" (as reported by Human Rights Watch).

Ghanaians have made enormous and sagacious strides in their collective quest for the democratization of their nation-state, the preceding having drawn unbridled praise from notable Western leaders. In fact, the relative peace, tranquility and interethnic co-existence Ghanaians have enjoyed under John Kufuor [president of Ghana from 2001 to 2009 and chair of the African Union during 2007–08]—even while Jerry Rawlings [Ghanaian leader from 1979 to 2001] should be fully credited with the genesis of this contemporary, Fourth-Republican democratic experiment—must be protected at all costs, as are the duties of the citizenry. It is for this reason that Ghanaians will be very displeased with John Kufuor, if the latter allowed Omar al-Bashir, a bigot, murderer, tyrant and criminal, to step on Ghanaian soil come October 2008.

I reiterate my appeal to the Gentle Giant [Kufuor] to heed the call of Ghanaians to reject Omar al-Bashir's plans to visit the Ghanaian capital, in order to show the rest of the world that Ghana's leaders would not condone human rights abuses, either on Ghanaian soil or elsewhere. If Omar al-Bashir is seeking legitimacy for his floundering and repressive administration, I suggest that he and his Janjaweed apparatchiks [loyal subordinates] rather celebrate their last days together before the sledgehammer of justice is unleashed—very soon—on them, for the Sudanese tyrant should receive no such approval from Ghana's John Kufuor.

China's Economic Interests in Sudan May Hinder Darfur Peace Efforts

Vivienne Walt

According to the following selection, one of the great ironies of the humanitarian crisis in Darfur is that it is happening at the same time that the nation of Sudan is undergoing an economic boom. The boom, based primarily on Sudan's oil, has been expansive enough to bring great prosperity to the Sudanese capital of Khartoum; it has even granted opportunities to Darfurian refugees and inspired emigrants to return home. Vivienne Walt, the author of the selection, writes that the key to the boom is demand from China, one of the world's newest industrial and economic superpowers. China's investment in Sudan not only ignores the alleged atrocities committed in Darfur; some claim that, in effect, China is financing those atrocities both for its own interests and those of Sudan's leaders. By contrast,

SOURCE. Vivienne Walt, "A Khartoum boom, courtesy of China," *Fortune*, August 6, 2007. Copyright © 2007 Cable News Network LP, LLLP. A Time Warner Company. Reproduced by permission.

Western nations have maintained economic sanctions on Sudan or refuse to do business there, in order to pressure leaders into dealing with the crisis. Some human rights activists went so far as to suggest that China's Beijing Olympics in 2008 be boycotted due to China's alleged connection to Darfur. Vivenne Walt has written for *Time* magazine and other publications since 2003. Her work focuses on African and Middle Eastern issues.

Late last year [2006] Adam Ibrahim Ali and his two teenage sons fled their ravaged village in Darfur and headed for Sudan's capital, Khartoum, riding on trucks and walking for days under the blistering desert sun. When they arrived in this dusty city on the Nile, Ali fashioned a small mud shelter on the riverbank and hung up his most cherished possession, a small transistor radio.

His escape from the four-year war in western Sudan turned out to be a smart financial decision. As the 115-degree heat eases in the evenings, Ali and his sons make bricks and bake them in the kiln next to their shelter to sell during the broiling afternoons. On good days they can earn about $12—enough for them, Ali's two wives and his 11 other children languishing in Darfur's biggest refugee camp. "We lost everything in the fighting," says Ali, 35. "Here we can sell bricks. People need them to build."

> Thousands of miles from the tough talk in Washington . . . and from Hollywood's celebrity campaign to save Darfur, Sudan is booming.

A Building Boom in Sudan

One glance at the city beyond Ali's makeshift home shows why he's doing a brisk trade. Thousands of miles from the tough talk in Washington about sanctions and peacekeeping troops, and from Hollywood's celebrity campaign to save Darfur, Sudan is booming. Cranes loom over Khartoum's cityscape while bulldozers roar down below, churning up the earth to make way for multilane roads and tall office buildings.

Think of Sudan these days and you're likely to envision janjaweed [roving gunmen, translates to "devil on horseback"] militia in Darfur rampaging through villages on horses and camels, killing and raping, or shallow desert graves and refugees in a scorched landscape. Those images have filled newspapers and television screens for more than four years. Yet during those same years billions of dollars have poured into Sudan—a rural country the size of Western Europe—thanks to a nascent oil industry whose production soared just as oil prices hit record highs and energy needs rocketed for Sudan's main customer, China.

The realization in the West that China's investment in Sudan might be financing the Darfur massacres has transformed a small activist organization on U.S. campuses into the biggest divestment push since the 1980s, when a similar campaign helped end white rule in South Africa. So fast has the political wave hit that without an international deal, it could cause the boom in Africa's largest country to wobble and overshadow China's biggest event in years, the 2008 Beijing Olympics. That has caused jitters in both Beijing and Khartoum.

"They are starting to wonder, 'How far can this go?'" says John Prendergast, a divestment activist and former director of African affairs at the National Security Council. "Sudan totally dismissed sanctions nine months ago. Now it is a different ball game."

Revitalization

Sudan's boom—not its anxieties—is obvious the moment one lands at Khartoum International Airport. The airy new hall opened a few months ago and is filled with foreign oil workers and business consultants. (A sprawling new $500 million airport is scheduled to open in 2011.)

Just beyond the airport perimeter, a showroom for Toyota SUVs opened this year, as did Khartoum's first Western-style luxury hotel, built by Abu Dhabi's Rotana hotel group. Guests at the hotel, now three-quarters full, can sip $5 cappuccinos in deep Italian sofas in the marble lobby or watch movies on large-screen TVs in air-conditioned rooms.

"There's a lot of cash and investment coming in," says Imad Elias, Rotana's executive vice president, at a cocktail party in the ballroom one evening. "Sudan is a place we want to be."

Downtown, construction crews are finishing an even more sumptuous hotel. Weeks from opening, the 19-story Al Fatih Tower on the riverfront is already Khartoum's most stunning landmark, with a soaring, curved façade in the shape of a dhow [Arab boat]. It is a rough imitation of Dubai's iconic Burj Al Arab—a telling reflection of Khartoum's grand ambitions. The owners are racing to open the $80 million hotel, financed by the Libyan government, on the Sept. 1 anniversary of Muammar Qaddafi's revolution.

> The Darfur crisis has shelved the possibility of resumed Western trade.

The top-floor restaurant offers a bird's-eye view of the transformation of Khartoum, which stands at the confluence of the White Nile and Blue Nile. Across the street stands a half-completed suspension bridge that will span both rivers. On a huge plot of land a new economic district with office buildings, villas and hotels is being constructed from scratch.

Real estate prices in Khartoum have skyrocketed: Studios rent for $1,000 a month, more than the yearly income of an average Sudanese. Sudan inked a peace deal in 2005 with non-Muslim rebels in southern Sudan—

site of most oil reserves—ending a 21-year civil war and turning the city of Juba into a boomtown too, with a new airport, hotels and banks.

"We are still very underdeveloped compared with places like Kuwait and Cairo," says Mujtaba Muhammed, a young Sudanese architect working on the Libyan hotel. "With all this construction, there is a lot of work for me."

A Checkered Past

This was not supposed to happen. Sudan was once a haven for Islamic extremists, including Osama bin Laden, who lived here until the government expelled him under U.S. pressure in 1996. The State Department declared the country a state sponsor of terrorism in 1993.

Then, in 1997, President [Bill] Clinton ordered sanctions, pushing out Chevron, General Motors, and other U.S. companies. The relationship hit its lowest point in 1998, when American jets strafed a Khartoum pharmaceutical factory, believing it to be an al Qaeda training camp. Officials frequently cite that attack as evidence of Western belligerence, and the hard-line Islamic government has left the bomb damage untouched.

Sudan aimed to break out of its isolation when it signed the peace deal with southern rebels. Officials repeatedly cast their country as a beacon of peace—a jolt for visitors. "We are a model for Africa and the world for being able to resolve our disputes," Vice President Ali Osman Taha told African intelligence directors at a Khartoum conference in June.

But the Darfur crisis has shelved the possibility of resumed Western trade, especially since U.S. officials first declared the massacres a genocide in 2004. Congress passed new sanctions legislation last year. And in late May, President [George W.] Bush and the U.S. Treasury banned 31 Sudanese companies from American and international financial systems. They include petroleum and telecommunications companies as well as the DAL Group, Sudan's largest private consortium, which bottles Coca-Cola and distributes European-made Caterpillar trucks, and whose construction company is building Khartoum's new economic district.

So far the European Union hasn't imposed similar sanctions. Yet that hardly matters to most European executives, who fear being tainted as supporting an abusive regime. "Sudan is politically radioactive for multinational companies," says Philippe de Pontet, Africa analyst for Eurasia Group, a U.S. risk consultancy. "The reputational risk outweighs any benefits."

Investors' Fears

That is likely to remain the case as long as reports of Darfur's killings persist. The conflict began as a local rebellion in 2003 that quickly scored victories against poorly equipped government forces. With patchy control over his vast country, President Omar Hassan Al Bashir backed Darfur militia groups to put down the insurgency.

Now Khartoum says it cannot rein in the fighters. In July, U.S. officials said, it resumed aerial bombing of Darfur. The UN estimates that more than 200,000 people have died and 2.4 million have been rendered refugees. (Sudan's government puts the death toll at about 9,000.) After decades of civil wars and Al Bashir's tough rule, Sudan ranked No. 1 on this year's "failed states" list compiled by the Carnegie Endowment for International Peace in Washington—above disaster zones like Iraq and Zimbabwe.

> Sudan earned more than $4 billion last year from petroleum exports—about 80 percent to China.

Yet by some measures this most-failed state is a big success. Its economy grew about 9 percent last year, and foreign investment rose to about

$5 billion, the second highest for an African country. The growth is overwhelmingly driven by oil, which accounts for most of the nation's GDP [gross national product]. Production has risen from 160,000 barrels a day in 2000 to about 480,000 barrels now.

Sudan earned more than $4 billion last year from petroleum exports—about 80 percent to China. With oil trading above $70 a barrel, residents say sanctions are hurting the West more than Sudan. "America is the loser," says Muhammed, the architect for the Libyan-built hotel. "They've given a great chance to Chinese companies."

The oil boom has lured home from the U.S. and Europe some Sudanese émigrés whose families had left a seemingly dead-end economy. Most days you can find some returnees at Khartoum's hippest café, OZone, which serves cinnamon muffins and iced caffe lattes. Ahmed Badawi, a British economist of Sudanese parentage, arrived last year to start a business and risk consultancy.

Two years ago Waleed Babiker quit his job in Minneapolis and returned to his native Khartoum, from which his family had emigrated ten years before. "My parents felt there was no possibility of making money," he says. Babiker now runs a travel agency, betting that Sudan's ancient pyramids will draw tourists once sanctions are lifted. His latest venture is a guide to Khartoum, which has advertisements for new cafés, Asian restaurants, and in June—get this—a pop concert in Khartoum to aid Darfur's victims. "We think this is a good time to make money here," says Babiker.

Friends to the East

That underplays the boom's big weakness: Sudan's fortunes depend heavily on a single customer, China. Its other partnerships, with Malaysia's Petronas and India's ONGC Videsh, are far smaller than the one with China National Petroleum Corp. [CNPC], which owns more than 40 percent of the Greater Nile Petroleum Operating Co., Sudan's largest oil firm.

Desperate to fuel its galloping economy, China has moved through Africa underwriting multibillion-dollar contracts for oil, gold, copper and other minerals. Unlike Western oil giants, it has also built power grids, telecommunications towers, highways and railway networks across the continent, ensuring its place as a major African benefactor.

Sudan is still only Africa's sixth-largest oil producer, far smaller than Nigeria and Angola. But China has a unique deal here: It faces no competition from Chevron or Royal Dutch Shell. As a result, China seems to be everywhere. CNPC's headquarters on Nile Street sits between grand government mansions built by Sudan's old British rulers and a hotel where Winston Churchill stayed.

> China's presence has the feel of a new colonial power.

Indeed, China's presence has the feel of a new colonial power. In the hotel lobby, next to a Christmas tree gathering dust in the blazing June heat, an eight-foot sign proclaims EVERGREEN FRIENDSHIP BETWEEN THE PEOPLES OF SUDAN AND CHINA. Nearby is the Chinese-built Friendship Hall conference center. Khartoum now has a school for Chinese workers' children and Chinese-language classes for Sudanese.

At dawn near the Rotana hotel, hundreds of Chinese construction workers clamber off buses to begin 12-hour shifts building a new headquarters building for Sudapet, Sudan's national petroleum company. Many of them gather Thursday nights at CNPC's headquarters for karaoke or to play in the Chinese basketball league. The Zijing Center, a Chinese travel agency and supermarket, is stocked with produce flown in weekly from Beijing.

"I go to the airport about three times a day to take Chinese people to flights or meet others arriving," says Jiang Lei, director of the travel agency. Air China plans to begin direct flights to Khartoum, which Jiang predicts will fill up quickly.

Khartoum, Sudan's capital, is experiencing a building boom due in large part to China's investment in its rising oil industry. (**Marco Di Lauro/Getty Images.**)

After years of clashes with U.S. politicians, officials are thrilled. "We are getting support without conditions from China," says Finance Minister Elzubair Ahmed Elhassan in his office late one night in June. "There is a feeling of fraternity and equality with them."

When Chinese President Hu Jintao visited in February, hundreds of people lined the route from the airport to greet him, and a camel was slaughtered in his honor. While Hu pledged $5.2 million in aid for Darfur refugees, he avoided scolding Al Bashir for the conflict in Darfur, wrote off $80 million in debt and offered $13 million in interest-free loans—including for a new palace for his host.

China, in fact, is digging in. In June, CNPC signed a 20-year concession for offshore drilling. In 2004 it spent $1.4 billion building a 1,000-mile pipeline from southern Sudan's oil fields to Port Sudan on the Red Sea, where there is also a new Chinese-built refinery. China's biggest project yet is the $2 billion Merowe dam north of Khartoum, which will more than double Sudan's power supply when it opens next summer.

An hour's drive out of the capital is a refinery, built in 1998 by Chinese workers in a joint venture between Sudan and CNPC. It looms over an arid plain amid camels and adobe villages and produces about 100,000 barrels a day of liquid gas and jet fuel. Inside the signs are in Chinese, and Chinese workers in blue overalls cycle around the facility. "We have a very strong relationship with Sudan," says Zhao Yujun, the refinery's technical manager. "And now that Sudan is booming, we are pleased to be contributing."

Second Fiddle

Yet for all the talk of friendship, officials concede they would readily swap China's affections for the West's. "It was not our choice to look East," says Hamed Elneel Abdel Gadeir, deputy secretary general of the Ministry of Energy and Mining. "But when we looked West, all the doors were closed." That has cost Sudan dearly, despite China's generosity and political allegiance.

The oil industry operates far below capacity, with imperfect equipment, according to oil analysts and government officials. "America has the largest oil companies in the world, with the expertise and experience," says Mahdi Ibrahim, former ambassador to Washington and a ruling-party leader.

Bashir Badawi, an advisor to the energy ministry who began his career as a Chevron geologist, says production would soar without sanctions. "We would hit three million barrels a day within eight to ten years," he says. "If U.S. sanctions don't lift, we will ultimately see declining production."

Sanctions bite in smaller ways too. Sudan is a cash-only country, with no credit cards or ATMs. And since no one can legally import U.S. goods, companies sneak in American products via third countries at higher cost.

That could be slow to change, given the furor over Darfur. In the past year 13 U.S. states have passed divestment laws, pledging to sell stock in PetroChina, whose parent company is CNPC. Last month Fidelity Investments offloaded most of its PetroChina stock, worth billions of dollars. And Warren Buffett, PetroChina's second-biggest investor after the Chinese government, survived a shareholders' divestment challenge in May.

China's Appetite for African Oil Grows

The campaign has hit China hard and rippled as far as Khartoum. Sitting in the Zijing travel agency, Liu Wugue, director of Chinese Petroleum Logistics in Sudan, says fear is growing among the Chinese that politics will spoil the Beijing Games. "Please don't link the Olympics to politics," he says. "It is our big chance. Until now the world knows China only from its products."

China is scrambling to control the damage. It dispatched a special envoy to Sudan to coax Al Bashir into accepting international peacekeepers for Darfur—a bottom-line demand from Western negotiators. After months of outright rejection, Al Bashir said yes to China.

Divestment alone might not be enough to end the killing in Darfur and bring millions of refugees home to their villages. That is likely to take long negotiations and thousands of UN troops. But if peace comes and the sanctions movement unravels, Sudan will finally open to

Western business. Officials say they are eagerly awaiting that day.

And Adam Ibrahim Ali, the Darfur refugee baking bricks on Khartoum's riverfront, says he and his sons also have plans. "As soon as there is peace," he says, "we are going home to Darfur." Until then he will listen to the roar of bulldozers erecting bridges and office buildings across the capital.

China Is Playing a Beneficial Role in Sudan's Development

Salah Nasrawi

In the following selection, the author discusses China's economic ties to many African countries, including Sudan. Unlike Western countries interested in the resources of these African countries, China avoids pressuring the nations on their political and human rights records. Although the author discusses critics' belief that China's arms exports have fueled conflicts within African nations, Chinese assistant foreign minister He Yafei believes their economic ties have helped improve Sudan's human rights record and facilitated its economic growth.

C hina's premier has begun a seven-nation African tour to sign deals to keep Africa's natural resources flowing to its booming economy and shore up support among its allies in its diplomatic rivalry with Taiwan.

SOURCE. Salah Nasrawi, "China Premier Begins 7-Nation African Tour," AP Online, June 19, 2006. Reproduced by permission.

Sudanese president Omar al-Bashir (left) accompanies China's president Hu Jintao (center) during Hu's tour of Africa. Chinese officials maintain that China's investment in Sudan reduces the violence in Darfur by decreasing poverty in the nation. (Isam Al-Haj/AFP/Getty Images.)

On Sunday [June 18, 2006], Chinese Prime Minister Wen Jiabao wrapped up a two-day visit to Cairo after meeting with Egyptian President Hosni Mubarak and signing 10 oil, natural gas and telecommunications deals. He also agreed to give Egypt a $50 million loan and a $10 million grant to encourage investment in an industrial area northwest of the Gulf of Suez.

Wen then headed to Ghana, where he signed an agreement to lend the small West African nation about $66 million to fund a number of projects. One is a plan to upgrade Ghana's communications network by increasing phone lines and improving the country's Internet system.

He was also scheduled to visit the Republic of Congo, Angola, South Africa, Tanzania and Uganda on the tour.

China and Africa

China has taken a keen interest in Africa's oil and minerals as its economy heads into a fourth year of 10 percent growth. Earlier this year, Chinese President Hu Jintao signed a series of major business deals with Nigeria, Africa's biggest oil producer, as well as an oil exploration contract with Kenya.

China is also striving to maintain its diplomatic contacts on the continent, as Taiwan steps up its efforts to gain international recognition—mostly among Third World countries. China and Taiwan split amid civil war in 1949, but Beijing still considers the island part of its territory and demands that its diplomatic partners give no formal recognition to Taipei.

Both Egypt and Ghana stressed their commitment to Beijing's "one China" policy.

China's headway into the continent has generated some criticism. Unlike Western countries also interested in Africa's markets and resources, China steers away from pressuring nations on their human and political rights records.

"This is not its concern. Business is," said Khalil al-Anani, an analyst with al-Siyassah al-Dawliyah, an Egyptian political quarterly published by the semiofficial Al-Ahram daily newspaper.

He said, however, that China's investments in African countries are mostly in state-run infrastructure projects. "These are long-term investments into which Western businesses probably do not want to venture," he said.

China's Relations with Sudan

Critics also have said that China's arms exports to some war-torn African nations have helped fuel conflicts, including the one in Darfur, Sudan, which has claimed at least 180,000 lives and forced more than 2 million people from their homes over the past three years.

But a top Chinese official defended his country's expanding relations with Sudan as "mutually beneficial." China's Assistant Foreign Minister He Yafei said earlier this month in Beijing that his country's dealings with Sudan have helped to improve that country's human rights records.

> "China's Assistant Foreign Minister He Yafei said earlier this month in Beijing that his country's dealings with Sudan have helped to improve the country's human rights records.

"It delivers tenable benefits to the Sudanese people and certainly facilitates Sudan's economic growth and its improvement of its human rights record," he said.

China's oil firms began investing abroad in the late 1990s, after double-digit economic growth outstripped supplies from domestic fields. In the last five years, the communist nation's trade with Africa has grown fourfold, to $40 billion in 2005.

Trade between Egypt and China alone topped $2 billion in 2005—four times what it was in 2002. China is funding 186 projects in Egypt, with a total investment of $220 million.

Wen denied that China wants to improve relations with Africa to control energy resources, saying its oil deals with African nations were open and transparent. He is expected to sign energy deals with some of the other countries on his current tour, though China has not provided more details on what these will entail.

Angola, Wen's fourth stop, is China's biggest African supplier of oil, accounting for 14 percent of total imports.

The United States, and the World Community, Must Continue to Act to End the Crisis in Darfur

Barack Obama

The following selection is a statement on Darfur made by President Barack Obama in October 2009 announcing that his administration was setting forth a comprehensive policy on Darfur. The United States was to continue to support the Sudanese government's efforts to bring peace and stability to the region, and he introduced the possibility of lifting some of the economic sanctions on Sudan then in place. The president hoped, furthermore, to build on agreements already in place, such as the Comprehensive Peace Agreement between the Sudan Liberation Army, one of the prominent rebel groups in Darfur, and the Sudanese government. He also reiterated the importance of the efforts of the United States' Special Envoy to Sudan, General Scott Gration.

SOURCE. Barack Obama, "'We Must Seek a Definitive End' To 'Genocide' in Darfur," in whitehouse.gov, October 19, 2009.

Today, my Administration is releasing a comprehensive strategy to confront the serious and urgent situation in Sudan.

For years, the people of Sudan have faced enormous and unacceptable hardship. The genocide in Darfur has claimed the lives of hundreds of thousands of people and left millions more displaced. Conflict in the region has wrought more suffering, posing dangers beyond Sudan's borders and blocking the potential of this important part of Africa. Sudan is now poised to fall further into chaos if swift action is not taken.

> Our conscience and our interests in peace and security call upon the United States and the international community to act with a sense of urgency and purpose.

Our conscience and our interests in peace and security call upon the United States and the international community to act with a sense of urgency and purpose. First, we must seek a definitive end to conflict, gross human rights abuses and genocide in Darfur. Second, the [2005] Comprehensive Peace Agreement between the North and South in Sudan must be implemented to create the possibility of long-term peace. These two goals must both be pursued simultaneously with urgency. Achieving them requires the commitment of the United States, as well as the active participation of international partners. Concurrently, we will work aggressively to ensure that Sudan does not provide a safe-haven for international terrorists.

The United States Special Envoy has worked actively and effectively to engage all of the parties involved, and he will continue to pursue engagement that saves lives and achieves results. Later this week, I will renew the declaration of a National Emergency with respect to Sudan, which will continue tough sanctions on the Sudanese Government. If the Government of Sudan acts to improve the situation on the ground and to advance

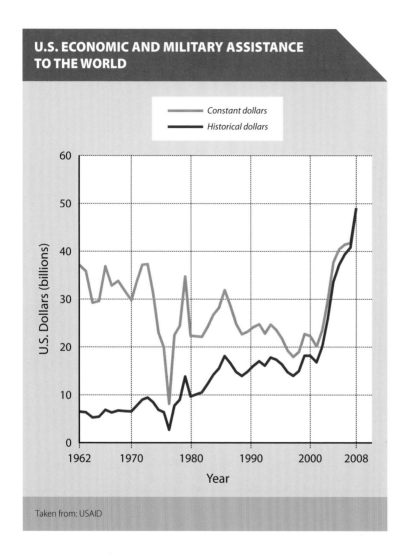

U.S. ECONOMIC AND MILITARY ASSISTANCE TO THE WORLD

Taken from: USAID

peace, there will be incentives; if it does not, then there will be increased pressure imposed by the United States and the international community. As the United States and our international partners meet our responsibility to act, the Government of Sudan must meet its responsibilities to take concrete steps in a new direction.

Over the last several years, governments, non-governmental organizations, and individuals, from around the world have taken action to address the situa-

tion in Sudan, and to end the genocide in Darfur. Going forward, all of our efforts must be measured by the lives that are led by the people of Sudan. After so much suffering, they deserve a future that allows them to live with greater dignity, security, and opportunity. It will not be easy, and there are no simple answers to the extraordinary challenges that confront this part of the world. But now is the time for all of us to come together, and to make a strong and sustained effort on behalf of a better future for the people of Sudan.

Photo on previous page: Sudanese refugees stream across the border to the neighboring country of Chad. Millions of Darfurians have been displaced by the violence. **(Scott Nelson/ Getty Images.)**

CHAPTER 3

Experiencing the Crisis in Darfur Firsthand

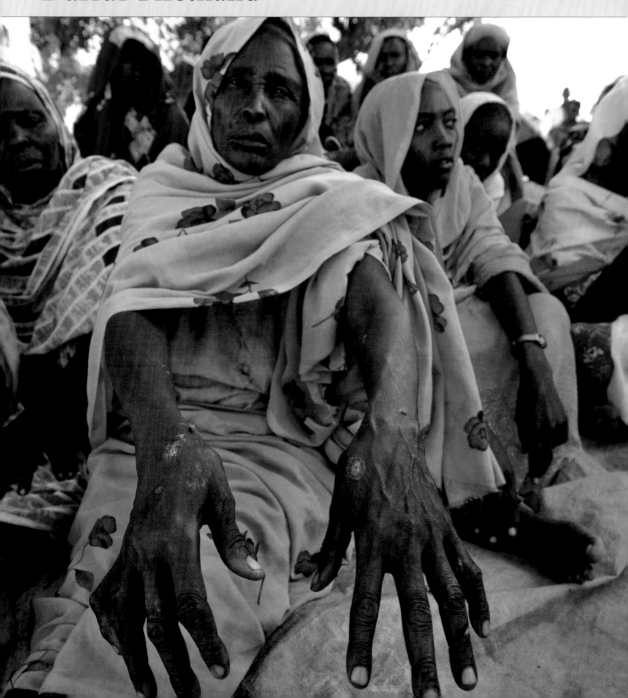

A Young Girl Becomes a Darfur Refugee

Nadia el-Kareem

In the following selection a young Darfurian woman tells the story of how the violence in Darfur changed her life. When she was thirteen years old, a group of mysterious attackers came to her village. While her brother saved her, she never knew what happened to her parents. After escaping to Sudan's larger cities and eventually to relative safety in Egypt, Nadia was married to Mahmoud, another refugee many years older than she. The couple eventually had a daughter. Despite the possible risks, Nadia wanted to "close her file" with humanitarian agencies and return home to Darfur.

My name is Nadia el-Kareem, and I was born on March 7, 1990. My tribe is the Masalit. I was born in Greda, a village in Darfur. I do not know where in Darfur. I have no education, and I don't know north, south, east, or west. I know my village is

Photo on previous page: A woman reveals the scars she received during an incident involving government soldiers. (Susan Schulman/Edit by Getty Images.)

SOURCE. Nadia el-Kareem, "Out of Exile: The Abducted and Displaced People of Sudan," *Voice of Witness*, 2008. Copyright © 2008 McSweeney's. All rights reserved. Reproduced by permission.

close to the town of Nyala. It's a small village of normal people. People go to their jobs and then come home again.

My father would go out to the farm and then come back to his house to stay with his children. It was not his own farm. It belonged to an old man I saw only once in my life. My father was not an educated man.

My mother was just a housewife. She had to cook, and she had to take care of her kids. Sometimes she took the cows out to eat grass. She was smiley, she chatted a lot with people, and she hugged a lot.

> The experiences I have had now are enough to make me forget everything about my childhood.

I don't know where my father is or where my mother is, but on my way to Egypt I met a lady who said she knew my parents. She told me, "Your father and mother died." I have two sisters and people have told me they are also dead. I have one brother. I saw him die.

I had a normal life like any girl in Darfur. I would help the cows and goats get food and water. I would clean the house and help my mother cook. I was happy. People who can stay with their parents should be happy. My cousin Muna was my best friend. We didn't really play together, but we would do chores around the house together, and when we finished we would sleep. Since the conflict, I have no idea where Muna is either.

That is all I can tell you about my childhood. The experiences I have had now are enough to make me forget everything about my childhood.

The Voice of Guns

It was 2003 or 2004. I was not yet fourteen. My father was coming from the farm, and my mother was outside with the cows. I was cleaning the cows' pen. My mother came back from the field and she yelled to me, "Did you finish?" because she wanted to get the cows inside. At the same time, my father was coming back from the farm. My mother got the cows inside the pen and closed the door. My mother and I went outside together to greet my father. My brother and sisters were inside the house.

Three or four men came, wearing something around their heads. You could only see their eyes. They were armed. They were running on foot and they were holding guns. I don't know if they meant to shoot us, but they did shoot another man and his wife who were our neighbors. The armed men were speaking, but I was scared and didn't hear them. I didn't understand what they were saying. My parents told me I needed to run. They called my sisters and told them to run.

I had heard of armed people coming and shooting before. I had heard the voice of guns many times, but I had never seen anything like this before.

I saw the men shoot children from the village. A boy was playing. They shot him also. I don't know why. All of us just ran away. I was just thinking about how to run away.

It was a messy moment. My father was holding his work tools and running. We were running very fast, and we met another group coming from the opposite direction. It was another group of people fleeing the place. Everyone was confused and I don't know how, but this was when I lost my mother and father. My brother, Mohammed, took my hand, and we started running with the new group of people. We ran away to a quiet place. We tried to hide. I was trying to hide myself, and my brother was watching the area to see if people were coming to attack us.

Two or three people showed up. They looked the same, with covered heads and covered arms. Mohammed told me to hide behind a tree. They didn't see me. I hid myself well. It was a big tree and I made myself small. When they moved to one side of the tree, I moved too to hide myself. Mohammed kept watching. Then they shot my brother from the back, and they ran away. Two shots. Then they ran away.

Mohammed was bleeding. I tried to wake him up, but he didn't move. I tried to hear his breathing—nothing. I tried to make him talk—nothing. So I moved. I ran. I kept crying, running, and crying and running.

I ran for maybe fifteen minutes. I met a man named Mahmoud and his brother. I hadn't seen them before. Mahmoud said he was also from Greda. He asked me, "Why are you crying?" I told him that my brother had died. They asked me, "How do you know he's dead? Maybe he's still living." I explained to them that I tried to hear him breathing and he didn't move.

We started running together. We ran for about two hours. We kept running, and they held me sometimes to keep me running. Mahmoud's brother said we would run to Nyala. It was my first time ever leaving my village.

Mahmoud is not short, not tall, not fat. Darker skin. A very normal, kind person. He's maybe thirty years old. He was very confused and scared like me. They were all afraid like me.

In Nyala, we arrived at the central station, and I met a woman I had seen during the attack. I asked her, "You were with us when the people attacked?" She said yes, and I asked her about my parents and about my sisters. The woman said to me, "I saw that your parents and one of your sisters had been shot."

They Said It Was Not To Be

Mahmoud's brother had some money to take us on a lorry from Nyala to Omdurman. We just jumped on the lorry and they drove for so long. I remember I was very thirsty. I was traumatized and I just kept crying, but I didn't feel anything really. I can't even remember how long they drove. I just remember getting out of the lorry at Omdurman. Mahmoud and his brother woke me up and said, "We have arrived. We have to get outside."

A view of the town of Nyala near where the author, Nadia el-Kareem, lived. (Mustafa Ozer/AFP/Getty Images.)

I saw a big city outside: stores for cold drinks, many people walking in the street, and many cars. The first thing I said was, "Where are we now?" They told me. "You are in Omdurman now." I asked him, "What shall we do here? I need my parents."

We went to live in a neighborhood called Dar-es-Salaam. Mahmoud's brother arranged the place. It was a room made out of mud with a small yard in front of it. Soon we had to leave though. I remember that one of the neighbors told Mahmoud and his brother, "You have to leave this place." Mahmoud went to the head of the neighborhood committee and spoke with him. I don't know the reason, but they advised him to leave the place. So we did. We went to live in a neighborhood called Khartoum Bahri. Mahmoud and his brother knew someone there, and that person helped get them a passport. They planned to go to Egypt.

I refused to go with them. I said, "What's my relation to you?" Also, it's illegal to travel with two men, to sleep with them in a house, and so on. All of this would cause trouble with the people and the government. In Sudan it's prohibited for an unmarried woman to travel with two men who are not relatives. They were definitely going, though. So I said, "Let's do what we need to do for this to be legal." Mahmoud said, "You are worried what the people will say about you for traveling with strange men." I said, "I don't care about the people. It's just not the right thing to do." Mahmoud said he would solve it. He said, "If you won't walk with strangers, then let us marry." Mahmoud was a normal age for Sudanese men to marry, but I had never heard of a girl my age, a thirteen-year-old girl, getting married.

We met a Sudanese man in the neighborhood and explained our story to him, and he agreed to act as my father for the ceremony. Then we went to a man responsible for making a marriage contract, and I was married to Mahmoud. The man gave Mahmoud a copy of the contract, and he gave a copy to me. But we stayed as normal. Mahmoud and his brother slept in one place, and I slept in a different place.

It was just in order to help me flee the country. Then they could put my name on Mahmoud's passport as his wife. If his passport says I'm his wife, then it's okay; there's no problem for me to travel or to be with him.

> Part of me wanted to return to Darfur, to search for my parents.

In total, we were in Khartoum and Omdurman for less than a month. Of course, I was still scared. Sometimes at night I couldn't sleep. I recalled all the experiences. I saw images of killing, and I had nightmares. I heard the voices of the guns, and I would wake up and cry at night. No one ever explained to me why it all happened. I couldn't understand a reason for myself.

Still part of me wanted to return to Darfur, to search for my parents. Mahmoud and his brother reminded me that the woman in Nyala said that my parents and a sister were dead. I said I could search for my other sister at least and stay with her. They said if I returned I might be killed also. They said it was not to be. . . .

It's Just Better to Die in My Country

Right now, in August 2007, the lady with the villa [where I work as a cleaning lady] is in [the Egyptian city of] Sharm el-Sheikh on holidays. Before she left, she gave me three hundred pounds (US$55) until she returns. But she said after she returns to Cairo, she will soon move to Kuwait. When she told me this, I explained my problems to her, told her about UNHCR [United Nations High Commission for Refugees] and everything. When she heard it, she said, "If you want to go back to Sudan, I can buy a plane ticket for you and a train ticket for your husband to travel to Khartoum. And if you stay here in Cairo, I will give you about six or seven hundred pounds." She tried to advise me: "If you make your mind up to go back to Sudan, please stay in Khartoum. Don't go to Darfur because you might face the same fate as your family."

> 'Don't go to Darfur because you might face the same fate as your family.'

Just last week Mahmoud and I went to UNHCR one more time. This time we went to close our refugee files. If you repatriate to Sudan, they say UNHCR will give you train tickets, and maybe one hundred dollars each to help you in your first few weeks.

At UNHCR they asked us, "Why do you want to close your file?" I told them there is nothing here for me and I am suffering. They asked us, "Where are you going to live in Sudan?" My husband said in Khartoum. I said I would rather go back to Darfur. The officer—Hisham was his name—Hisham said, "If you will go to Darfur, I cannot close your file." And then Mahmoud said, "For sure, we will go to Khartoum."

Hisham asked us to sign some papers. He said to Mahmoud, "Call me this afternoon, and I will give you an appointment to go to the interior ministry." Finally, two days later, we got the appointment. Mahmoud had to go to the Ministry of Foreign Affairs first. They gave him a paper to take to the Ministry of the Interior, in order to get us an exit visa.

Now Mahmoud has a job for a few days, helping an old woman move some things. The job finishes tomorrow, and he will go to the ministry to see if we have a visa. We will go to UNHCR again to get assistance for closing our file. The lady with the villa will be back in a few days, and I will find out if she will help. It will be difficult, because she wants to give me tickets to travel, but UNHCR wants to give us train tickets also. The lady has given me a lot, and I don't want to press her to change her offer.

I am very ready to go back to Sudan. There are no benefits to going back, and I know there could be risks. I still want to go to Darfur, even though it's dangerous. Even in Khartoum there might be security risks. But it's just better to die in my country, in my home.

I have no feelings about UNHCR at this point. They did nothing for me. They didn't offer anything. They didn't help me. That is all I think. But I feel nothing. The same for Egypt. I live here, eat, and sleep like any eighteen-year-old. But Sudan is my country. What happened to my family was the work of criminals. It was the Sudanese government's mistake not to secure the lives of the Darfurians. But Sudan is my country. I hope the Sudanese government takes care of its citizens, and I hope UNHCR pays more attention to the refugees.

In Sudan, I will live in the same circumstances as here in Cairo. Nothing new will happen. I think my daughter's life will be the same as mine—no education, no nothing. We will all just stay like this.

I guess I still have some hope. I haven't been there before—I have no experience about this—but I have hope to go to America or Australia. Everyone tells me that you can find a safe life there, and your daughter can find a good education. That would be a hope. Education and a stable life. I know in Sudan that will be impossible. And

I know if I go back to Sudan, I will not get to Australia or America. But now it's all the same to me. If I can find work in Sudan, I will work in Sudan. If I can find food, I will feed my daughter. If I die, I die. Life, death, there's no big difference. God will make it easy.

Watching Soldiers and Refugees Come and Go

Jen Marlowe with Aisha Bain and Adam Shapiro

In 2004, three activists from the U.S., Jen Marlowe, Aisha Bain, and Adam Shapiro, traveled to Darfur to document the experiences of ordinary people there. They eventually produced both a documentary film and a book titled *Darfur Diaries: Stories of Survival*. The following selection is part of one such story, an interview with a man named Dero in his village, Shegeg Karo. A teacher and English speaker, Dero recalls attacks from both Janjaweed militias connected with the Sudanese government as well as the rebel Sudanese Liberation Army. He also mentions seeing much suffering and urging refugees to flee to safety in nearby Chad. Despite the strife and instability, Dero maintains hope, even expressing tentative hopes for marriage. Jen Marlowe is a filmmaker, author, and producer deeply involved in humanitarian causes. Aisha Bain is Asia Program Coordinator at Global Rights: Partners for Justice. Adam Shapiro is an activist

SOURCE. Jen Marlowe with Aisha Bain and Adam Shapiro, *Darfur Diaries: Stories of Survival*. Cambridge, MA: Nation Books, 2006. Copyright © 2006 Jen Marlowe, Aisha Bain, and Adam Shapiro. All rights reserved. Reprinted by permission of Nation Books, a member of Perseus Books, L.L.C.

and filmmaker as well as a doctoral candidate in international relations at American University in Washington, DC.

W e arrived in Shegeg Karo in the late morning where we were told we would stay until after iftar [the evening meal]—at least five hours. Dero looked happy to be back in his home village. It seemed like a lifetime ago that we had first met Dero in Shegeg Karo. I couldn't believe it was just under a week.

"Do you want to see my school?" Dero asked us, ducking his head modestly.

"Of course! We'd love to!" Aisha said.

He led us through the market to the hut that had been the school. It was where the teenaged Fadi had so eagerly inspected the old rocket launcher. Last week, I hadn't noticed the blackboard leaning outside of the hut.

"So you built and ran this school yourself?" Aisha asked, with some amazement.

Dero rubbed his teeth with the frayed ends of a stick. "Yeah, because no school here in Shegeg Karo. There are more than three thousand people in this area without any school, any hospital. You see now. After I left secondary school, I couldn't go to university. I returned back here to build this school, to run it by effort. No one paid me. I tried to call to people to pay for their children so I could teach them. I didn't care about age. If someone came, more than twenty years, or seven, or eight. My aim was not about age. I wanted to educate people how to read and write. I taught three years without any salary, but after three years this war happened, and now we stopped. I stopped teaching."

Dero took us inside the hut. It was dark, but our eyes adjusted with the help of the light filtering through the cracks in the walls built with mud. Dero painted a picture for us, using his tooth-brushing stick as a pointer.

> 'If the war is over and the situation gets better, I can try to build a school again.'

"The blackboard was there. And the students sat on the ground. Sometimes more than thirty in one class, sometimes less. I tried to teach them how to read and write the alphabet in Arabic. I tried to teach them a few words of English." Dero shrugged, his life's work now abandoned. "Now they use it as a base of the SLA [Sudanese Liberation Army]."

"And will you build a new school?" Adam asked, filming the interior of the hut.

"Yeah, if the war is over and the situation gets better, I can try to build a school again. I will call those who have some education to teach the people here." Dero nodded thoughtfully, rubbing his teeth repeatedly with the stick. "Yeah."

An Ancestral Visit

When we were last in Shegeg Karo, the old sheikh had told us we could find the graves of his ancestors on top of the nearby mountain. We asked Dero if he would take us there now. With the cameras slung over our shoulders, we started to climb the narrow, rocky path that led to the top of the mountain. We passed clusters of stones lined up and organized in a certain pattern. There were no markings.

"These are more recent graves," Dero explained, showing us how they were aligned to point toward Mecca, in accordance with Muslim burial practice.

We made it to the top, slightly out of breath. We saw huge piles of earth-colored stones and smaller gray and white rocks scattered on the ground. Even without marking, Dero knew exactly which graves were connected to which family. He led us to the rock-covered graves of his own ancestors, which he touched reverently, as well as to the oldest graves on the mountain.

"These graves are from before the time of Islam," he told us.

The view from the top of the mountain was spectacular. A large valley of green and brown patchwork lay below. Trees, rocks, and desert stretched for miles in every direction. Dero stood at the edge of the cliff for a long time, gazing silently at the expanse of his ravaged homeland.

Finally, he turned and nodded to us. "Let's go back to the market," he said softly.

We followed him down the rocky mountain path. Dero led us to the same stall where we had sat the day we met him. There was a woman peeling small red onions with a large, sharp knife and tossing them into a black cauldron over a fire. A baby boy with hair that formed a perfect mohawk was strapped with a piece of cloth onto her back. She welcomed us into the space. Dero agreed

Conditions were so bad in Sudan that many refugees were forced to cross into neighboring Chad to find greater security. (**Scott Nelson/ Getty Images.**)

to talk on film. We knew as we set up the camera that this interview would be different from any other. We had laughed with Dero, sung with him, ridden miles with him across the desert. He was our friend.

Dero began by telling us about the baby and his mother. The boy's father had been killed alongside Dero's brother. He described what happened.

"We depend on our animals. We have here only camels, sheep, cows. There is no agriculture or maize. In southern Darfur, there are many farms. They would bring their maize to Deesa on market day. And we would sell our animals to get what we need: food, clothes, or anything from market. The father of this boy went with his animals on market day to Deesa last January, accompanied by my brother. Suddenly the janjaweed [roving gunmen, translates to "devil on horseback"] surrounded the market and killed all the people—hundreds of people killed in one day."

No one spoke for a moment. I wondered whether the atrocity had even been covered in the news. "How did you learn about the attack? Did somebody tell you or did you hear something on the radio?" I finally asked.

A Lost Brother

"No, no, no, not the radio," Dero answered, looking down and shaking his head. "We haven't phone, but after about five or six days we heard the news that many people were killed on market day in Deesa. And then I began to worry about my brother. Yeah. I tried to tell my mother that he was not killed with them, that he was spared, that he is not what we call *shaheed* here, I don't know in English. . . . "

"Martyr," I told him.

"Martyr." Dero mulled the word over in his mind for a moment. "I wanted them not to worry about it. I tried to comfort her—console or condole?"

"Console," I said gently.

"Console," Dero repeated the word, trying to commit it to his memory and then continued. "We waited for more than ten days, and when my brother didn't return, we were sure he was one of those people killed. My mother became crazy, crying all the day, not eating, not drinking. She became ill and thin. My father was patient, not like my mother. Somehow . . . but not like my mother.

"The government troops stayed in Deesa more than six months after the murder. We couldn't go to bury. When the area was liberated by the SLA, I went to search for my brother's body. I couldn't know which was my brother or others, because all the bodies were damaged and destroyed. We couldn't tell by appearance. We gathered all of them and we buried them in Deesa."

Dero began peeling small pieces off the stick he had been rubbing against his teeth earlier.

"You buried everyone together in one grave?"

"Yeah. We could not know the details of who was who." There was silence again. Dero broke it first. "Now when I remember, I feel very bad. It was very hard for me to hear my brother killed in the market without any reason. But there is nothing I can do. Sometimes I remember many times in one day. Also, about this kid's father." Dero pointed to the toddler boy. "Now, when you are asking about my brother, I am also thinking about this kid. His mother needs clothes, food. No one gives it to them. Yeah, I'm thinking about this and about my brother every day. I am feeling very bad now."

"Does it help you to talk about it?"

"When I talk about my brother, I feel very hard. I can't more, I can't more than. . . . " Dero didn't finish his sentence. "Yeah." We sat without speaking as Dero arranged the shredded pieces of his stick into rows.

"Why did you choose not to fight with the SLA?" Aisha asked what we were all wondering.

"Because of my father and mother. There is no one to take care of them here. We were only two brothers. If my brother were alive, I could join the SLA. But if I participate in fighting, maybe I would be killed and my mother and father would have no one to take care of them. But I support them in other ways, when it's possible."

"Can you tell us a little bit about your mother and your father?" Aisha asked.

"My father used to have many animals, camels, cows, and sheep.

My brother, as I told you, looked after the animals. He brought them to market and brought them hay, grass. But now all the animals died because no one takes care of them. And now my father is very poor. He doesn't have any livestock. My father is more than sixty years old. He can't walk to look after animals. My mother is also more than sixty years old. And that is taking all my attention, how to take care of them, how to make a better situation for my parents. I wanted to go with them to a refugee camp, but they refused. They said to me that they don't want to cross to Chad."

"Why do they refuse to go to the refugee camp?" I asked.

"I don't know. They said they don't want . . . they die here, not in Chad. This is their home."

"But you wanted to go to a refugee camp?" I continued.

"Yeah, if it was possible, because there are no food and services here. It's very hard here. If they would come to the refugee camp, it's better, but they refused."

Escaping to Chad

Very hard here, Dero said, but as he began to speak about the Darfurians fleeing into Chad, his description was harrowing.

"I tried to forget that tragedy. But I can't. Last October, in Shegeg Karo, you had to pass this road to cross to Chad. I saw children die here, suffering, no food. Many people crossed from here. I saw the tragedy. All the people who you saw in the refugee camps in Kariare, in Iridimi, most of them crossed from here. They were walking on their foot and sometimes they didn't have food, they didn't have water. Some of them tried their way and they died in the desert, thirsty. Many tragedies.

'They were walking on their foot and sometimes they didn't have food, they didn't have water.'

"I felt very, very sad at that time. Sometimes I tried to get water from the well for these suffering, thirsty people. Sometimes I gathered food from my family to give people. But other times I went to another village. I couldn't stay here to see the tragedy. If I didn't have anything to give them, I couldn't watch them crying, thirsty and dying. I had to go away. I couldn't see them like this."

"Do you ever feel angry?" I asked.

"Now angry," Dero answered softly and gently. "If I remember my brother, I feel very angry and sad."

"Do you want revenge?"

"Revenge?"

"When someone hurts you so you want to hurt them back," I explained.

"No, no, no, no. I would try to explain to him that it's wrong. What he's done is wrong. If you have anything against me, you can deal with it, not by killing or by hard thing. You can use another way. Yeah."

"If you saw the one who killed your brother, what would you do?"

He spoke softer still, reconsidering his response, perhaps. "I can fight with him."

"What do you hope for your future, Dero?" Aisha asked.

"I hope to find a good job to take care of my parents."

"What is a good job?" Aisha asked.

"Any work, any salary."

"But what do you dream of doing?" Aisha pursued.

"I dream of being a schoolteacher. If I have the chance to study more, that would be good, but this chance to study is not available. So I try to find work to look after my parents."

"What kind of work do you find?" I asked.

"There is no possible work here now. I tell people to hide."

"Hide from what?" I questioned.

"Like the airplane that you saw this morning. If I gathered students in this school to teach them and suddenly the airplane came to bomb it, then that would be wrong of me. Because of that I call to people to go to Chad or to hide."

"What did you feel when the airplane came yesterday?"

"I feel some fear. But, *al-hamdulillah* [praise to God], there was no bombing."

"Did you help translate for a lot of journalists before us?" Adam asked.

"Yeah, some journalists come here. I try to help them, to show them the facts and accompany them on their trip, because there are no hotels. They need someone to take care of them. For me, it's good for many reasons. First, I can show all the world what is happening here. Also, I improve my English. And sometimes they give me some fee. Yeah. If it's possible." He avoided our eyes intentionally, not wanting to appear as if he was dropping a hint. "But it's not enough. Because my English is not good. Sometimes I try to explain more, but I can't."

"What would you study if you could?" I asked.

"I want first to improve my English, because English is important to study anything else, anything modern. And then, if it's possible, medicine. Because all this area, from the border of Chad until Kutum, there are no doctors here, no surgery, no medicine."

"Do you want to get married someday and have kids?" I asked.

"In this situation, no. It is a very hard life and I can't take more responsibility. No."

"Is there some special girl you know?" Adam asked.

"Maybe, sometimes, I . . . " Dero broke off, laughing and blushing.

Aisha, Adam, and I exchanged grins. "Sometimes?!" Aisha teased him.

"Yeah." Dero tried to meet our eyes but began giggling again and looked down bashfully.

"Does she have a name?" I wanted to know.

"I cannot . . . ," he laughed again and shook his head.

"How many camels do you need to marry her?" Aisha joked. "Usually it would be ten, or more than ten," and then he added with uncharacteristic swagger, "but if I am to marry her, I don't need camels!"

"If you do, you must give camels to us . . . " I began with Aisha finishing my sentence.

"For compensation!"

The four of us laughed, enjoying this playful moment together, knowing there wouldn't be many more before we left Dero behind in Shegeg Karo as we continued into eastern Chad. And with the video camera on, we had to capture Dero in his finest moment.

A Playful Moment

Aisha set the stage. "Dero, what's your favorite music?"

"My favorite is Bob Marley because he's revolutionary."

"You like which song?" she prodded.

"Sit up, sit up don't give up your right . . . stand up for your right . . . don't be survive." Dero attempted, getting the tune mostly right. "Yeah, that song very good for me."

"Can you sing a little 'Buffalo Soldier' for us?"

"Um . . . " Dero paused, considering the request. He eyed the mother of the little boy with the mohawk. She was stirring soup in the black cauldron, eyeing him back.

He laughed, embarrassed. "No, there are many people looking at me."

Aisha didn't give up so easily. "Come on, man." She began singing the song herself, special Dero-style. "*Oi yoi yoi. . . .*"

Dero jumped right in without any further encouragement, clearly enjoying himself. "*Oi yoi yoi yoi!*" he continued after Aisha backed out of the singing, giving us his full rendition with gusto. "*I sing on arrival, I sing for survival. A stolen map of Africa in the war on America! I sing on arrival! I sing for survival! Oi yoi yoi!*"

We cheered and clapped when the performance was finished. "*Kor kadai!* (Very good!)" Aisha praised him with a few of the Zaghawa words she had picked up.

When the laughter died down, the discussion turned serious again. "Dero, if you do get married and have kids someday, will you tell them about this time in your life?"

"No," Dero said firmly. "I not tell them this story, because it's very . . . this story can affect him in his mind. People now in Darfur are suffering mentally because they saw many, many crimes. Many people not normal now because they are suffering in their minds from these problems, what happened in Darfur. And so I can't tell to my kids these stories. It's very hard."

> In every war-torn area I have been, I have met extraordinary people who are able to hold onto their dignity and humanity.

His answer surprised me. In other communities that have experienced collective trauma, including other Darfurians, we were told that the telling of the story to the next generation—so the memory lives on—is of paramount importance. Dero was, we continued to discover, unusual in so many ways.

"You said many people lost their minds," I repeated.

"Yeah."

"You did not. You are still so sociable and kind and gentle. . . . "

"Yeah." He met my gaze head-on. I wasn't sure if he fully understood what I meant.

"You have managed to keep yourself alive inside of you."

"Yeah."

In every war-torn area I have been, I have met extraordinary people who are able to hold onto their dignity and humanity after living through and witnessing unimaginable horrors. I don't know how they are able to. Adam, Aisha, and I, sitting in front of Dero, were humbled by him.

"*Habibi* [my friend]. Thank you for telling us your story," I said.

Escaping Ahead of a Village Attack

Brian Steidle with Gretchen Steidle Wallace

The following selection is a part of a recollection of Darfur written by Brian Steidle, a former U.S. Marine officer who served as an American military observer to the African Union's peacekeeping force in Darfur in 2004 and 2005. Steidle, along with other observers and monitors, from the United States and elsewhere, visited Darfurian villages by road and helicopter, learning firsthand of attacks by government Janjaweed militias as well as attempts by local people to fight back. His account includes a story of a narrow escape in a damaged helicopter from the village of Jayjay. Brian Steidle, along with his sister Gretchen Steidle Wallace, is the author of *The Devil Came on Horseback: Bearing Witness to the Genocide in Darfur*. He is also a photographer, filmmaker, and activist.

SOURCE. Brian Stiedle with Gretchen Steidle Wallace, *The Devil Came on Horseback: Bearing Witness to the Genocide in Darfur*. Cambridge, MA: Public Affairs, 2007. Copyright © 2007 by Brian Stiedle and Gretchen Steidle Wallace. All right reserved. Reprinted by permission of Public Affairs, a member of Perseus Books, L.L.C.

The next day we flew to the villages of Gireida, Joghana, and Jayjay, all part of the province of Gireida, one of the last tribal kingdoms in Sudan. The king of Gireida, Abdulrahman Bokhit, was of higher rank and importance than the GOS [Government of Sudan] appointed governor of all of South Darfur. He even had his own private GOS police detachment to provide him with security. The fact that these GOS security men were protecting him was not an indication that the GOS itself was aligned with the king. In fact, the king was of an African tribe, but he had been able to remain neutral and maintain peaceful relations with all sides in the conflict until now. There had been no fighting inside his kingdom until an attack that occurred three days earlier in Jayjay.

We landed first on the airstrip next to Gireida to meet with the king. He arrived dressed in a brilliant white jelabia [traditional Arab garment] and surrounded by his military police detachment.

"There has been an attack on our village of Jayjay. I also have received a letter from an omda [village mayor], warning that the Janjaweed [roving gunmen, translates to "devil on horseback"] will attack Gireida next," he reported. "I have ordered my police unit to arrest the militias and have called on every man in the province to come to defend his kingdom. They are to meet in Joghana this morning. You must go there and help them."

Before we departed, the king presented me with the cane he was carrying. He shook my hand, remarking that he had never met an American before. He said that he respected our country greatly and wanted me to remember him. I thanked him as we turned to leave.

Joghana was the next stop. We touched down outside the village, where a large group of 300 people with guns, spears, and vehicles had gathered. They told us they were waiting for us on instruction from the king to take representatives of our team to meet with a group of omdas and sheikhs assembled in the village. The townspeople could only transport two monitors and our interpreter in their small pick-up truck. I volunteered to go, and Dave [another American observer], with us for the day, decided to join me as well.

A Scary Gathering

They drove us into the central marketplace where a group of around 300 people were yelling and cheering. I felt a bit alarmed, wondering if they were celebrating our capture. They led us to an empty cement building that was guarded by three dump trucks filled with men carrying spears, swords, and guns. Inside the building it was bare except for a metal desk and a few chairs.

Within moments, several omdas and sheikhs entered the building and sat down with us. They provided more detail about the fighting in Jayjay.

"Around 30 Janjaweed on horses and camels attacked the village," a sheikh began. I suspected this was possibly an out-of-control Janjaweed force involved in a local dispute because the GOS was not involved in this attack.

"Our village defense force fought off the militia forces and successfully captured their leader, Mohammed. When we got him, he had been driving a car that belonged to the government-appointed mayor of Buram." The mayor had evidently lent him his vehicle to use in the attack.

"Now the militias are preparing to strike back and free their leader. The king has called on all residents to defend Jayjay. These are the people gathering outside. We are preparing to take them to the village by truck." We ended our meeting quickly and returned to our helicopter so that we could fly to the site of the conflict.

We touched down into chaos. A vehicle immediately screeched to a halt alongside our helicopter. We could see a man in the rear of the pickup truck bed with a gunshot wound to the leg. Blood was streaming down his calf, and people all around us were yelling. A group of women had gathered and were waving their hands in the background. Apparently, the villagers had not had water in three days. The Janjaweed were holding their water hole. The women were demanding that their men go retrieve water.

> 'I'm going to go kill some Janjaweed.'

An old man about 65 or 70 came up to us in a white jelabia and flip flops. He was holding a huge spear, nearly ten feet long with a massive head on it. Through Ibrahim [an interpreter], I asked him about his spear. He said he last used it in 1976. I asked where, and he replied that he had killed an elephant with it.

"Whoa," I responded. "What are you doing with it now?"

"I'm going to go kill some Janjaweed," he said and walked into the bush.

More Shooting

The local civilian defense force brought the Janjaweed leader to us. He was beat up. I felt no emotion when I saw him with his arms shackled behind his back. We began asking questions but were immediately interrupted by gunshots in the distance—perhaps 2 kilometers away. The fighting had resumed, and we suspected the Janjaweed were moving on the village. Villagers of all ages were emerging from their huts with axes, spears, clubs, or anything they could find that could serve as a weapon. Ahmed and I looked at each other with eyes wide.

"They are going to get their water hole back," Ahmed said.

We heard more shooting, closer now. Anour and Ibrahim jumped up immediately. No one needed to say, "Let's go." We dashed back to our helicopter and loaded up as the pilots started the engine. The engines turned over briefly but then cooled down again. Another try, another failure. The pilots screamed back to us that they could not get the second engine started. The gunshots continued in the distance.

We all got out of the helicopter and looked around us. We were in a wide field of sorghum stocks, the earth hard as a rock. At that instant, I heard the firing of a rocket propelled grenade. The Janjaweed were getting closer. Dave looked at me.

"Well, we may be the only two white people to ever witness a Janjaweed attack firsthand," he said. "Only we won't survive to tell the tale."

Dave pulled out a satellite phone and called our operations room.

"We're in Jayjay," he yelled. "It's crazy here. You've got to get us out of here. We're about to get caught in the middle of a Janjaweed slaughter, and the damn helicopter won't start. We need a maintenance crew and as many protection forces as you can fit in our other chopper."

Dave's face went white and he turned off his phone. He relayed the news, "They'll be there within an hour."

"Within an hour?" I shuddered. We looked around, wondering what we could do when all hell broke loose. As soon as the militia poured into our field from the higher grasses beyond, all they would see would be a huge white helicopter. We had no weapons and couldn't even dig a hole.

We could see women in the village loading their belongings onto donkeys and fleeing in the opposite direction. All the men and boys, even as young as eight years old, were preparing to fight. There was no apparent strategy. Some men were heading into the field, while others were positioning themselves in front of their huts. I watched the scene in horror. They had no chance.

A Tense Wait

Minutes passed. Dave and I sat there and said nothing; all the while the gunfire was getting louder. My heart beat in my throat. I looked at my watch. It had only been ten minutes. I swore I could hear Arabic voices shouting through the grass. I looked at Ahmed. He was kneeling by the helicopter with the other Muslim monitors praying. Joseph was pacing back and forth, holding his hand to his forehead.

Finally, we heard chopper blades in the distance. Ibrahim and Ali cheered and jumped up and down. I let out a huge breath and made the sign of the cross. A helicopter roared into sight. Three pilots, a few maintenance guys, and 10 protection forces jumped out when it landed. The new crew brought a machine gun, which they positioned at the head of a semicircle the Rwandan soldiers formed in front of our two helicopters. We weren't out of trouble yet, but we were in a much better position.

Two Russian maintenance workers opened the engine compartment on top of the helicopter and climbed up into the hood. One of the guys with a 10-pound sledge hammer began bludgeoning the engine. He yelled down to the pilot, who then started up the engine as the Russian continued pounding away. I could not imagine how long this remedy would last.

"Dave, I don't know about you," I said, as a piece of machinery flew by me, "but that looks like a quick fix to me. How about we take the good helo back?" He nodded and I turned toward the mechanics.

"Listen, you guys take this one in case it needs any more work. We'll go on the chopper you came in. Let's split the protection forces between us," I instructed.

We climbed into the helicopter and slammed the door. I peered out the window and caught the eye of a tiny girl holding her mom's leg as she loaded her other children onto the back of a donkey nearby. "Jeez," I breathed to myself. "What's going to happen to them?"

As we lifted off from Jayjay we saw the three dump trucks from Joghana pulling in filled with more armed villagers. I felt only slightly reassured. They might be

> I couldn't imagine these men with spears and clubs could save their village alone.

able to hold off the Janjaweed long enough for their kids and wives to flee to safety, but I couldn't imagine these men with spears and clubs could save their village alone.

Our most experienced pilot was at the helm. He flew toward the fighting below tree level, swerving between nim trees. We could see some people dragging the injured back toward the village and others heading out into the conflict with axes and spears. Gunshots rang out all around us. The pilot decided to fly a bit higher so we would not risk getting shot. As we neared the Janjaweed forces, we could see a number of militiamen in offensive positions, others on camels and horses.

Suddenly, our pilot laughed and said, "Watch this." He pointed to a Janjaweed on a horse just ahead. Lowering the helicopter, he headed straight for the man. The militiaman looked over his shoulder and saw the huge helicopter heading his way. In fear of his life, he kicked his horse into a flatout gallop, trying to outrun our aircraft as we came closer and closer. We soared over the horse, nearly throwing the Janjaweed soldier to the ground with the force of our gust. The entire team cheered in the cockpit. But the high from this small victory was short-lived. It did nothing to compensate for what we knew would be inevitable.

We flew farther, toward the place where the Janjaweed forces had originated, identifying nomad settlements on the other side of the water hole. As we continued, we saw five or six more villages smoldering. The Janjaweed had been burning villages all along their way to Jayjay.

A Darfurian Doctor Plans to Continue Reminding the World of Her People's Suffering

Times Colonist (Victoria)

The following selection relates the story of Halima Bashir, a doctor from Darfur, who tells of not only her experiences in Darfur but of her desire to discuss them openly. The author of a book titled *Tears of the Desert*, Bashir was herself beaten and raped before eventually escaping to England. Despite discouragement from fellow Darfurian refugees, who felt that it might be shameful for her to speak of her sufferings, Bashir insists that the stories of Darfurian women be told.

They came for Halima Bashir at midday, to the clinic where the young Darfur doctor was tending to victims of atrocities committed by sanction of

SOURCE. "Survivor of Darfur Horrors Rejects Calls for Her Silence," Canada.com, September 21, 2008. Reproduced by permission.

the Sudanese government. She had hoped it was United Nations officials arriving with crucial medical supplies. Instead, three scruffy soldiers strode into the clinic and hauled her out of the building to a waiting jeep.

"My heart was pounding, pain drilling like a jackhammer inside my skull," she writes in her terrifying new memoir, *Tears of the Desert*. "I knew they were going to kill me."

But she was wrong. They didn't kill her. She was thrown into a cell in a military camp and beaten. She was kicked in the stomach and hit repeatedly on the legs, hips and shoulders. "I fell to the floor and tried to cover my head with my arms. A boot made contact with my face, a searing white light shooting through my eye socket. Another kick to the head, this one smashing into the fingers of my hand with the crunch of breaking bone."

> 'It is not our custom for Darfur women to speak out, even when they are the victims.'

The beating continued, and then she was moved to a detention hut and painfully bound and gagged. That night, government soldiers and members of Sudan's dreaded Janjaweed militia [roving gunmen, translates to "devil on horseback"] came and raped her repeatedly as she cried to her god for help. The gang rapes continued for the next three days.

Even now, talking to Canwest News Service in the sanctuary of her London publisher's office, Halima Bashir can barely bring herself to talk about those days. She is shy and reserved, speaking so quietly, you sometimes must strain to hear her. But you also sense a steely resolve—the resolve that compelled her to risk ostracism from her own Zaghawa tribal community by telling the truth about Darfur in her new book, written in collaboration with British journalist Damien Lewis and published in Canada by HarperCollins.

Fellow Zaghawan exiles were shocked when Bashir began speaking out publicly in 2006, a few months after her arrival in Britain.

Needing to Speak Out

"Even my closest friends didn't accept it. They said that everyone in the world knows what happened and that I added nothing to speak out about this—that it was shameful to do so, that it was not our custom."

She is sad about this but unrepentant. *Tears of the Desert* is the first memoir by a woman caught up in the conflict in Darfur, and it's in bookshops because she refused to be silenced by members of her own community or intimidated by the Sudan's Arab rulers responsible for what she condemns as appalling acts of genocide.

"When I first came to this country [England], I found that people had heard about what is happening in Darfur and what is happening to my people. And I felt a little bit relieved and happy, because so many people did care about the war in Darfur and were going to help us and support us."

But she became troubled by the fact that the information was almost all statistical. The public was aware of the bald facts: militants from non-Arab African tribes in Darfur had rebelled in 2003 against discrimination by the Arab-controlled Sudanese government, which then used its feared Janjaweed militia to crush the insurgency. Bashir wanted to go beyond those statistics—85,000 people killed, 200,000 dying of war-related diseases, more than two million displaced in what she sees as a calculated act of ethnic cleansing. She wanted westerners to understand the human dimension.

"There were no personal stories that had been told. It was also because the women are the weakest part in Darfur, and didn't get the chance to speak about the violence committed against them. It is not our custom for Darfur women to speak out, even when they are the victims.

"So, because I am a woman, I feel I have to do something for my people. And by writing the book, I feel I am doing something for the thousands of other Darfurian women who have suffered the same agonies."

But why had Bashir—a doctor who had been dispatched to a remote region because her services were badly needed—been singled for torture and gang rape? What specifically had she done to trigger the fury of the authorities? Simple: she had committed a grievous crime by telling a UN team about an attack on a girls' primary school and the raping of pupils as young as eight.

Young Victims

For Bashir, it was in many ways more painful to recount the physical and emotional damage done to these children than it was to recall the abuses she herself suffered. She had to steel herself in describing her emotions when she examined the first young victim and discovered the horrific extent of the injuries.

"At that moment, I didn't know exactly what to do. I felt horrified that I couldn't do anything to help. I was trying as much as I could to help them, but it was difficult."

What subsequently happened to her as an adult was appalling enough, but her heart goes out to those little girls.

"How much more painful for them, because they understand nothing. They'll never forget it for the rest of their lives."

Tens of thousands of women and girls in Darfur were subjected to rape and other forms of sexual violence—and agencies such as UNICEF and the Alliance For Direct Action Against Rape In Conflict and Crises continue to document new atrocities and to condemn the use of sexual violence as a war tactic as an offence against international law. That's why Bashir is overjoyed by the International Criminal Court's recent decision to charge

Sudanese President Omar Hassan al-Bashir with master-minding a campaign of genocide in Darfur.

"I can't explain to you how happy I was. We felt it was a significant step in bringing justice to Darfur. It is something that should have been happening a long time ago."

Bashir and her people are black. However, like their Arab extermina-tors, they are also Muslim. She says people need to realize that Darfur is not being torn apart by religious conflict—it is being destroyed by racism, pure and simple. And, the trauma of today is rooted in what happened when Sudan's British colonizers left the region.

> She will never, never forgive those responsible.

Ethnic Cleansing

"They gave the power to the Arab tribes to govern the country. And, of course, the Arab tribes are a small mi-nority and most of their areas are in the North, where there are not many natural resources and not much wealth, whereas most of our area has many resources. The Arabs control all that wealth, and then they decided to take our land from us. That is why there is fighting. They want to clean the land of any black African tribes."

The first part of her book describes a largely happy childhood for Bashir. Her father was a successful cattle herder and it was important to her to describe life before the terror.

"It's really important. Because, you know, my village has been destroyed, my people have been killed. There are special things you have to remember. That's why I describe my childhood—just to show we were living a normal, happy life. All of it is gone because of the war."

And she will never, never forgive those responsible.

"No, I won't," she says. Now her voice is firmer, stronger. "I'm thinking all the time about taking revenge.

I have to do it for the many innocent people who have been abducted, the women who have been raped . . . revenge for people killed. It's very difficult to forgive. I'm not thinking about forgiveness. There will be revenge one day."

CHRONOLOGY

1821	Egypt, then loosely tied to the Turkish Ottoman Empire, conquers much of Sudan, installing rulers loyal to Turco-Egyptian elites.
1875	Sudan's rulers overthrow the semi-independent state of (Dar)Fur in the west of the country.
1884	A revolt is led in Sudan by the Mahdi, a Messiah figure in Shia Islam. His followers conquer Darfur and defeat British colonialists, installing a strict Islamic regime.
1899	The Mahdi's government falls, and Sudan falls under the joint government of the British Empire and Egypt.
1916	Darfur is formally added to Sudan.
1955	The first Sudanese Civil War begins. Lasting until 1972, it pits, in general terms, the central government in Khartoum, dominated by Arab Sudanese, with black African separatists in the south of the country.
1956	Sudan gains its independence from the British Empire. The nation is governed as a centralized state under a "Native Administration" system which grants local autonomy to tribal chiefs.
1969	Gafaar Nimeiry becomes president of Sudan. From a northern Sudanese Arab tribe, Nimeiry remains in office until 1985 despite several coup attempts.
1970s	Arab militias seeking the creation of a larger Pan-

Islamic state in North Africa under Libyan sponsorship grow active in Darfur as well as in neighboring Chad.

1983 The Second Sudanese Civil War begins. It lasts until a peace agreement is reached in 2005.

1985 President Nimeiry is overthrown.

1987 Arabist groups begin to take up arms in Darfur, starting the first Arab-Fur war lasting until 1989.

1989 Omar al-Bashir becomes president of Sudan.

1990s Tensions rise between Darfur and the Sudanese government, resulting in the appearance of an armed resistance movement in Darfur.

1998 U.S. military aircraft bomb a pharmaceutical plant in Khartoum, ostensibly targeting Islamic extremists.

1999 Sudan exports its first shipments of oil.

2000 The Sudanese government develops plans to "marginalize" Darfur according to documents allegedly received by rebel groups.

2003 March: Two major resistance movements, the Sudanese Liberation Army (SLA) and the Justice and Equality Movement (JEM) make public their aims to resist the government and begin to launch attacks on government positions.

July–September: The first massacres in Darfur take place, carried out by government-backed militia groups.

September: The Sudanese government and the SLA begin peace discussions.

December: The Sudanese government launches a major offensive in Darfur, resulting in more massacres and tens of thousands of refugees.

2004   March: UN observers first refer to the massacres in Darfur as genocide.

April: A temporary ceasefire takes effect, calling for monitors from the African Union (AU).

June: The massacres in Darfur are called a genocide by the U.S. Congress.

July: The UN issues an ultimatum urging the Sudanese government to disarm the Arab Janjaweed militias in Darfur.

August: Peace talks are renewed between the Sudanese government and various rebel groups in Abuja, Nigeria.

September: The UN Security Council opens an International Commission of Inquiry on Darfur.

2005   January: The Second Sudanese Civil War comes to a formal end, as the government reaches an agreement with rebel organizations. Low-level hostilities continue nonetheless.

March: The UN recommends that the International Criminal Court review the atrocities in Darfur.

July: Sudan forms a Government of National Unity, although not all rebel factions take part.

November: Peace talks resume in Abuja, Nigeria.

2006   January: The African Union rejects the proposal to

choose Sudanese President Omar al-Bashir as its leader.

March: Both the government and rebel groups reject a continued ceasefire and return to fighting.

May: Demonstrators stage a major rally in Washington, D.C., urging the U.S. government to take action on the Darfur crisis. Participants include actor George Clooney, Holocaust survivor Elie Wiesel, and then-Senator Barack Obama.

May: The U.S. enacts sanctions against the Sudanese government.

May–August: A new Darfur Peace Agreement is reached in Abuja. It is rejected by the JEM and one faction of the SLA. The general rebel movement in Darfur continues to splinter as new groups emerge and some leaders join the Sudanese national government. Fighting continues.

2007   April: The International Criminal Court issues indictments against the first Sudanese government and militia leaders accused of war crimes in Darfur.

May: The United States extends its economic sanctions against Sudan.

June: Amnesty International releases *Instant Karma*, a collection of covers of songs by John Lennon by various musicians, many quite famous. It is intended to both raise money for and awareness of the crisis in Darfur.

2008   January: The UN takes over the peacekeeping mission in Darfur.

April: A UN observer estimates that as many as 300,000

have died as a result of the fighting in Darfur.

July: The International Criminal Court brings charges of genocide, crimes against humanity, and war crimes against Sudanese president al-Bashir. He rejects the accusations. An actual arrest warrant follows in March 2009.

November: President al-Bashir calls for a ceasefire in Darfur. Rebel groups reject it, insisting that the government grant South Sudan more self-government.

December: Fighting between the government and rebel groups extends into the region of Kordofan, which is rich in oil. The government blames Darfur-based rebels for creating instability in the region.

2009 July: Leaders of South Sudan agree to arbitration with the government over several contentious issues. The arbitration was to take place in The Hague, Netherlands.

August: The leader of the UN peacekeeping force in Darfur claims that the war in the region is over.

December: Various factions agree on the principle of a vote on Southern Sudanese independence to be held in 2011.

2010 January: President al-Bashir agrees to abide by the decision of any referendum on Southern Sudanese indendence.

March: The last of the major Darfur rebel groups, the JEM, reaches an agreement to end its fighting with the Sudanese government.

April: President al-Bashir is reelected in Sudan's first open, national elections in more than twenty years. Some question the legitimacy of the vote.

May: Clashes between the Sudanese government and rebels from the Darfurian Justice and Equality Movement result in dozens of deaths.

FOR FURTHER READING

Books

Benjamin Ajak, Benson Deng, Alephonsian Deng, and Judy Bernstein, *They Poured Fire on Us From the Skies*. New York: Public Affairs, 2006.

Halima Bashir, *Tears of the Desert: A Memoir of Survival in Darfur*. New York: One World/Ballantine Press, 2008.

Don Cheadle and John Prendergast, *Not on Our Watch: The Mission to End Genocide in Darfur and Beyond*. New York: Hyperion Books, 2007.

Robert Collins and J. Millard Burr, *Africa's Thirty Years War: Libya, Chad and the Sudan*. Boulder, CO: Westview Press, 1999.

M.W. Daly, *Darfur's Sorrow: A History of Destruction and Genocide*. Cambridge, UK: Cambridge University Press, 2007.

Alexander de Waal, *Famine that Kills: Darfur, Sudan, 1984–1985*. Oxford, UK: Clarendon Press, 2004.

Julie Flint and Alex de Waal, *Darfur: A New History of a Long War*. London: Zed Books, 2008.

Daoud Hari, *The Translator: A Memoir*. New York: Random House, 2009.

Chris Herlinger and Paul Jeffrey, *Where Mercy Fails: Darfur's Struggle to Survive*. New York: Seabury Books, 2009.

Douglas Johnson, *The Root Causes of Sudan's Civil Wars*. Oxford, UK: James Currey, 2003.

Leora Kahn and John Alter, *Darfur: Twenty Years of War and Genocide in Sudan*. New York: Powerhouse Books, 2008.

Mahmood Mamdani, *Saviors and Survivors: Darfur, Politics, and the War on Terror*. New York: Doubleday, 2010.

Gerard Prunier, *Darfur: A Twenty-First Century Genocide*. Ithaca, NY: Cornell University Press, 2008.

Abdel, Salam Sidahmed, *Politics and Islam in Contemporary Sudan*. Richmond, UK: Curzon Press, 1997.

Alex de Waal, ed., *War in Darfur and the Search for Peace*. Cambridge, MA: Harvard University/Global Equity Inititative, 2007.

Articles

Abdulmoneim Abu Edries Ali, "U.S. woman among three aid workers abducted in Darfur: Sudan," Agence France Presse, May 18, 2010.

Hillary Anderson, "China is Fueling War in Darfur," BBC News, July 13, 2008.

Anonymous, "Sudan Biggest Target for Chinese Investment in Africa," *Sudan Tribune*, March 28, 2007.

M. Calabresi, S. Dealy, and S. Faris, "The Tragedy of Sudan," *Time*, October 4, 2004.

Jeffrey Fleishman, "Sudan elections highlight north-south divide," *Los Angeles Times*, April 11, 2010.

Lucy Fleming, "Darfur: where celebrities love to tread," BBC News, February 9, 2010.

J. Fowler, "In Sudan, staring genocide in the face," *Washington Post*, June 6, 2004.

Warren Hoge, "Security Council Backs Darfur Peace Accord," *New York Times*, May 16, 2006.

Kasie Hunt, "Celebrities, activists rally against Darfur genocide," *USA Today*, May 1, 2006.

Nicholas Kristof, "Genocide in Slow Motion," *New York Review of Books*, February 9, 2006.

Anne McFerran, "Curse of the Janjaweed," *Sunday Times (UK)*, September 23, 2007.

Lydia Polgreen, "Attacks Pushing Darfur Refugees into Chad," *New York Times*, February 11, 2008.

John Prendergast, "A Dying Deal in Darfur," *Boston Globe*, July 13, 2006.

J. Ryle, "Disaster in Darfur," *New York Review of Books*, August 12, 2004.

Web sites

Darfurian Voices (darfurianvoices.org). The Web site of the organization 24 Hours for Darfur is devoted mainly to maintaining a video record of reactions to the Darfur crisis. It contains filmed statements from victims, observers, humanitarian activists, and others. It also features a blog.

Eyes on Darfur (eyesondarfur.org). A Web site maintained by advocacy group Amnesty International. It seeks to provide thorough evidence from many sources, including satellite imaging, of the extent of the crisis in Darfur.

Save Darfur (savedarfur.org). An informational Web site focusing primarily on governmental action, lobbying activities, and fundraising. It also offers up-to-date news and even an online shop.

Sudan Research, Analysis, and Advocacy (sudanreeves.org). Maintained by Eric Reeves, a university professor from the U.S. with a deep interest in Sudan. Contains maps, articles, and photographs and offers extensive links to other sources.

The Sudan Tribune (sudantribune.com). An English-language online newspaper offering up-to-date reports on Darfur and other matters related to Sudan. It also maintains an archive of documents and maps.

INDEX